ONE
HUNDRED&
ONE
REASONS TO GET OUT OF BED

TWIG²
PO Box 3005
Allambie Heights,
NSW 2100,
Australia

www.101reasonstogetoutofbed.com

ISBN: 978-0-9944628-0-0 (paperback)
ISBN: 978-0-9944628-1-7 (ebook)

Designer: Luke Jarman

FSC
www.fsc.org

MIX
Paper from
responsible sources
FSC® C014174

Printed in the United States of America

SMALL WORLD STEPS. BIG PLANET HEROES.

ONE HUNDRED & ONE

REASONS TO GET OUT OF BED

NATASHA MILNE & BARBARA ROYAL

Foreword

As I sit and reflect upon what to write for the foreword to 101 Reasons To Get Out of Bed, I wonder what I can say to stop the assault on my mother, The Earth. This is one of the hardest issues to address. This Mother, Our Earth, has sustained my tribal ancestry for millennia in one of the harshest parts of our globe, Central Australia, and now she struggles. As we go on taking from her with no thoughts of tomorrow, it is time the metaphor of the greedy caterpillar, who consumes all that it can, be turned into the butterfly. It is time now for us to go out and propagate what Mother Earth needs for her health to return, so she is able to care for us once again.

Time is of the essence, and so I ask that everyone read this very important book, inwardly digest it, and outwardly live a life in the service of and for the future of our Mother. I call on all humans who where born of our Mother Earth, to open your eyes, to see her beauty, be grateful for her love, respect her, nurture her, and defend her.

Do not be overwhelmed, do not despair, but find hope in the knowledge that you as one person have the ability, the responsibility, and the great opportunity to become a butterfly.

**Rosalie Kunoth-Monks,
First Nation Arrernte, Anmatyerre,
Alyawerr Central Australia**

ROSALIE KUNOTH-MONKS was born on the dry riverbed of the Urapuntja river at Utopia in Central Australia in 1937. She starred in the first color feature length film made in Australia "JEDDA". Rosalie was an Anglican Sister for ten years. In 1969 Rosalie left the order and married in 1970. She won the inaugural Dr M Yunupingu human rights award, is the 2015 Northern Territory Australian of the Year and the 2015 NAIDOC Person of the Year. Rosalie continues to advocate for a Truth and Justice journey with all Australians toward the greater goal of a Treaty.

This book is dedicated to those who wake up each day and work tirelessly for the betterment and survival of our Mother Earth. And to every one of us sharing this beautiful planet, especially those who cannot speak for themselves. May we all take small world steps to become big planet heroes- respecting, nurturing and preserving our only home.

101 Earth Advocates

Introduction

It seems like every day we are bombarded with doom-and-gloom stories of our planet in crisis. From wildlife poaching to oceans full of plastic, food safety to climate change, it sometimes feels hopeless. Increasingly I have found myself searching out stories that offer hope, stories about people who are working every day for the betterment and future of our only home—it's the stuff we don't get to hear about in mainstream media.

What I didn't count on was finding so many people making a difference. There are literally millions of people from every walk of life, consciously fighting for our earth. I wanted to highlight what these people are doing, but unfortunately, showcasing them all in one place would have made this a very big book, so instead, we asked just 101 people to tell us all what animal or environmental issue gets them out of bed and why, what they are doing about it, and if they can offer some tips to the rest of us.

From heroes like Dr. Jane Goodall fighting against ivory poaching to Jonah Cameron, a 10-year-old boy with a lemonade stand raising awareness for orangutans, each contributor has his or her own reason to get up in the morning. Some of the answers may surprise you, some may inspire you, and some you may not care for at all, but the theme that runs throughout is one of concern and respect for our planet and all her inhabitants, and an understanding of our individual responsibility to keep her alive and thriving into the future.

Although many of these reasons might seem unrelated, they are in fact parts of the whole interconnection between everyone and everything in this world. I believe that humanity is fundamentally good, and proof of this lies in seeing these 101 individuals' desire to help people connect with themselves, each other, and the planet through compassion, empathy, and ultimately action.

Barbara Royal and I hope that within these pages you'll be inspired to find your own *one thing* and act upon it. You will soon discover that your one thing becomes infectious. Far from being helpless, governments and corporations and even global consciousness will respond—you can literally change the world.

Let us all take small world steps to become big planet heroes.

Natasha

Introduction

E.B. White said, *"I wake up each morning with both the desire to change the world and the desire to enjoy it. This makes it difficult to plan my day."* This book has been extremely useful in getting me out of bed and helping me plan my day.

Since 1995, I have worked with pets, endangered wildlife, and exotic animals. I have seen extraordinary people do incredible things to save animals. I have been very lucky—I know the quiet gentleness of rhinos and have felt the curious bristles of a manatee's whiskers. I also know that all of us benefit from the efforts of people saving animals like these.

Natasha and I hope this book spurs conversation and inspires action to continue resolving even our most troubling global problems. Changing the way we view and manage our planet involves much more than a love of animals. It requires that we recognize our own power to be a force for health or sickness of the entire planet.

But this may feel overwhelming. In many cases we might think that it's too hard to change things—or maybe it's just too late. How can we fight resistant bacteria or cancer? How will farmers make food without pesticides, fungicides, and herbicides?

Some problems may not even be on our radar screen. On a dark night we are relieved to switch on a light, but is it possible that light pollution has an alarming affect on wildlife—and even our own mental health? And maybe some answers are just difficult to talk about, like composting toilets. While it's a topic to avoid at a dinner parties, we know that it's also foolish to take perfectly clean, precious water and defile it in a toilet.

Who finds these issues a reason to get up in the morning? Who can take on indoor plumbing and the electric light bulb? Unless we ask these questions, we may never know the answers. We want to share the stories of others who have moved past apathy in favor of achievable action. We know you are out there.

Some of the best advice I've received is that you can't do everything you want, but with a little focus you can do anything you want. If each of us chooses to focus on one or two environmental issues that we're passionate about, and if each of us accomplishes something, even a little something, that alone can change the world. So get out of bed and get going!

Barbara

What animal or environmental issue gets you out of bed, and why? We used to get our herbal medicine from the forest, then with deforestation, so many herbs disappeared, our soil is eroding, and the weather is changing. Once you could get a lot of produce from a small area, when there was no erosion. Farming land mass has shrunk and it is not so productive. People are leaving the rural areas and going to cities and other places. The climate is drier; rains are not as rejuvenating when they come. We thought modern fertilizers were the solution and at first, they seemed to work, but they do not in the long term. They ruin the land. Herbs that grow locally can stop and prevent the diseases in people and animals. I worry that our traditional medicines will disappear for future generations. Our herbs are so important.

What are you doing about it? I am a member of the Botanica Ehiopia project and the Etse-Fewus (or healing herb) garden association now. Through our association, the local government supports household gardens and provides our community with land to grow herbs at risk due to deforestation, land degradation, and loss of knowledge. The gardens flourish. The government has promised more land and our Botanica Ethiopia members have received permaculture training to learn how to increase soil productivity and conserve water. I go to other houses and talk about the herbs and the land with my friends. The association for the Etse-Fewus works collectively to show what can be done with our healing herbs. This has made me happy.

What can everyone do about it? We have to understand what we have lost and continue what we are doing now: planting gardens and trees and supporting groups that teach about natural herbs and natural ways to protect plants, the soil, and our water. If we work together, we can do more.

SHIKERKE ABABU is a householder who lives in Fiche, Ethiopia. With other men and women, householders and farmers, she is part of an association called Etse-Fewus, or Healing Herbs, which was formed with the support of a small organization called Botanica Ethiopia, whose research promotes and protects the local use of traditional herbal medicines. Its members have received permaculture training (Strawberry Field Eco-Lodge, Konso, Ethiopia) to increase soil productivity and conserve water.

What animal or environmental issue gets you out of bed, and why? The need to feed and tend to the many rescued farmed animals in my care gets me out of bed every day. (It also keeps me up late at night and keeps my clothes dirty!) I am passionate about animals, the natural world, and justice.

What are you doing about it? In 2003, I created Edgar's Mission, a not-for-profit sanctuary for rescued farmed animals. The sanctuary provides a safe haven for animals in need, and through our outreach work, farm tours, and humane education programs, we provide the public with an opportunity to experience the rich and emotional world of the animals our society farms for food and fiber. We aim to empower people with the knowledge that one person can make a difference. The broader scope of this work marries my sense of justice with my love of animals, my concern for the environment and my desire to see people fulfill their maximum potential. As a child, I had no idea of the terrible impact my lifestyle choices had upon my animal friends, the planet, and my health. I want children and adults alike to have access to the information that was denied to me by those in animal-based agriculture, government, and industries. I truly believe a humane and just world for all is but a kind choice away.

What can everyone do about it? Listen to your heart and ask yourself this very simple question: If we could live happy and healthy lives without harming others, why don't we make lifestyle choices that encourage the industry behind products to behave more humanely to animals?

PAM AHERN is the founder and director of Edgar's Mission, a not-for-profit sanctuary that provides a safe haven for rescued farmed animals. She gave up her day job and a successful equestrian career to dedicate her life to the protection of farmed animals. Pam was a Victorian finalist in the Australian of the Year Awards, Local Hero section, for her work as an animal rights activist. Edgar's Mission is set on 150 peaceable acres in the beautiful Macedon Ranges, Victoria, Australia. In ten years, thousands of farmed animals have been given a second chance at life after having made their way through the farm gates.

Jonathan Balcombe

What animal or environmental issue gets you out of bed, and why? The issue that frustrates me, excites me, and drives me forward is the profound disconnect between what we know about animals as sentient beings and our cruelty and indifference toward them. Most people object to animal cruelty, but fund it on a daily basis by their purchasing decisions. What we choose to eat especially has a huge impact on animals and the environment Change is happening. Today the options for living compassionately are flourishing. The last decade has seen a 10% decline in meat consumption in the United States. This trend must become global if we're to have a future worth living in.

What are you doing about it? As an ethologist (a student of animal behavior), I draw attention to the new science on animals' inner lives. Our scientific community is asking important questions about how animals think and feel, revealing exciting new aspects of emotion, perception, intelligence, communication and virtue. Here's a small sample: fishes play, crocodiles cooperate and use tools, parrots name their children, dogs monitor the emotions on our faces, starlings experience pessimism and optimism, wild chimps deactivate poachers' snares, fishes rate each other's good behavior, and wild lemurs engage in substance abuse. I give between 20 and 50 presentations a year and, with the Humane Society Institute for Science and Policy, we are forming a new journal, Animal Sentience, devoted to the science of animal feelings and designed to advance changes in policy and practice. Also, my books draw attention to animals' ability to feel pleasure and the moral implications of that.

What can everyone do about it? Engage. We need to keep our senses open and make good choices. Animal-friendly products are everywhere these days. In addition to the staples of fruits, grains and vegetables, today's supermarkets are stocking plant-based versions of everything from sausages to cheese to seafood to yogurt and plant-based milks. If yours doesn't, ask them to. Compassionate alternatives are also available online.

JONATHAN BALCOMBE is a scientist and author. He has published over 50 scientific papers and writes extensively on animal behavior and ethics. He is the author of three popular books: Pleasurable Kingdom, Second Nature, *and* The Exultant Ark. *Balcombe currently serves as Director for Animal Sentience with the Humane Society Institute for Science and Policy in Washington, DC. His next book,* What a Fish Knows, *is on the remarkable lives of fishes.*

What animal or environmental issue gets you out of bed, and why? I'm inspired by the many ways in which cities can be designed and planned to include nature, to emphasize the restoration of natural systems, and to foster profound connections with the natural world. As we increasingly urbanize the planet, we need to make sure that cities are biodiverse and nature-full. There is a growing global movement to recognize the importance of contact with nature and re-imagine cities with nature positioned at the center of urban living. We call these BIO*philic cities*.

What are you doing about it? Much of my research has been about studying and documenting the innovative ways that cities around the world recognize the important emotional need we have for contact with nature and have been integrating nature into their design and planning. These insights and stories are included in the books I write (including recent books *BIOphilic Cities* and *Blue Urbanism*), the documentary films we make, and in the university classes I teach. We have launched a new network of biophilic cities. Our aim is to build a global community of planners, urbanists, elected officials and citizens who will advocate nature in their cities and who will assist their counterparts in other cities by sharing of information, ideas, and insights about tools, initiatives and programs that have worked.

What can everyone do about it? Every individual and group living in a city can take tangible steps to grow nature, to help that city become more biophilic. It might be planting street trees, installing a butterfly garden, or organizing a weekly bird-watching walk. It can also involve advocating and pushing for biophilic design and planning at the neighborhood, city or regional level. City plans and policies can be strengthened to protect the nature that exists and to grow more nature in cities—from ecological rooftops to vertical gardens, managing light pollution and daylighting urban streams. And more ambitious goals and targets can be set for the future, such as imagining urban living environments in which urbanites are immersed in nature.

TIM BEATLEY, PhD, is the Teresa Heinz Professor of Sustainable Communities and chair of the Department of Urban and Environmental Planning at the University of Virginia, where he has taught for the last 28 years. Beatley is the author or co-author of more than fifteen books on urban planning and design. He is founder of the Biophilic Cities Project and co-director of the UVA Center for Design and Health.

What animal or environmental issue gets you out of bed, and why? I developed my initial love for nature and the great outdoors by following my dad around the bush as a young boy and learning from him. My dad was a farmer and a soldier, but he was an even greater conservationist—he taught me to think of ants as much as elephants. Today, I am a wildlife ranger. It is a great privilege to be an active part of the ongoing conservation effort to preserve one of the last true wilderness areas of Africa, the Kafue National Park. It is what gets me out of bed every morning.

What are you doing about it? My work in Kafue National Park began with the establishment of an Elephant Orphanage Project. We rescue, rehabilitate, and release orphaned elephants back into the wild. This has now grown into a fullfledged organization: Game Rangers International (GRI). Successfully releasing an orphaned elephant safely back into the wild requires that we embrace and support a holistic approach to wildlife conservation. We must include law enforcement, education, community outreach, research, and the ongoing training of wildlife personnel. It is my long-term goal, based on the successes and challenges we have experienced in Kafue, to develop a type of 'plug-n-play' conservation template that can be used to provide support to other vulnerable wilderness areas around the world.

What can everyone do about it? I believe there are three types of people: those who do nothing; those who speak a lot but don't actually do anything; and those who just get on with it, making a positive difference to the world and to people around them. The easy option is to do nothing. However, my guess is that if you are reading this book, then you fall into the last category and you have already made a decision, at some level, to do something. I encourage you to continue with this effort and to share this wonderful approach to life with your children—for they will feel the real differences of what we have done to this world.

SPORT BEATTIE is the founder and CEO of Game Rangers International, the project manager for the GRI–Kafue Conservation Project, and serves as the honorary warden for greater Kafue National Park. A native of Zimbabwe, he served in the British army and worked with elephants and game scouts in the jungles of Cambodia before returning to southern Africa. In 2007, with ongoing and critical support from The David Shepherd Wildlife Foundation, he established the Elephant Orphanage Project in southern Africa.

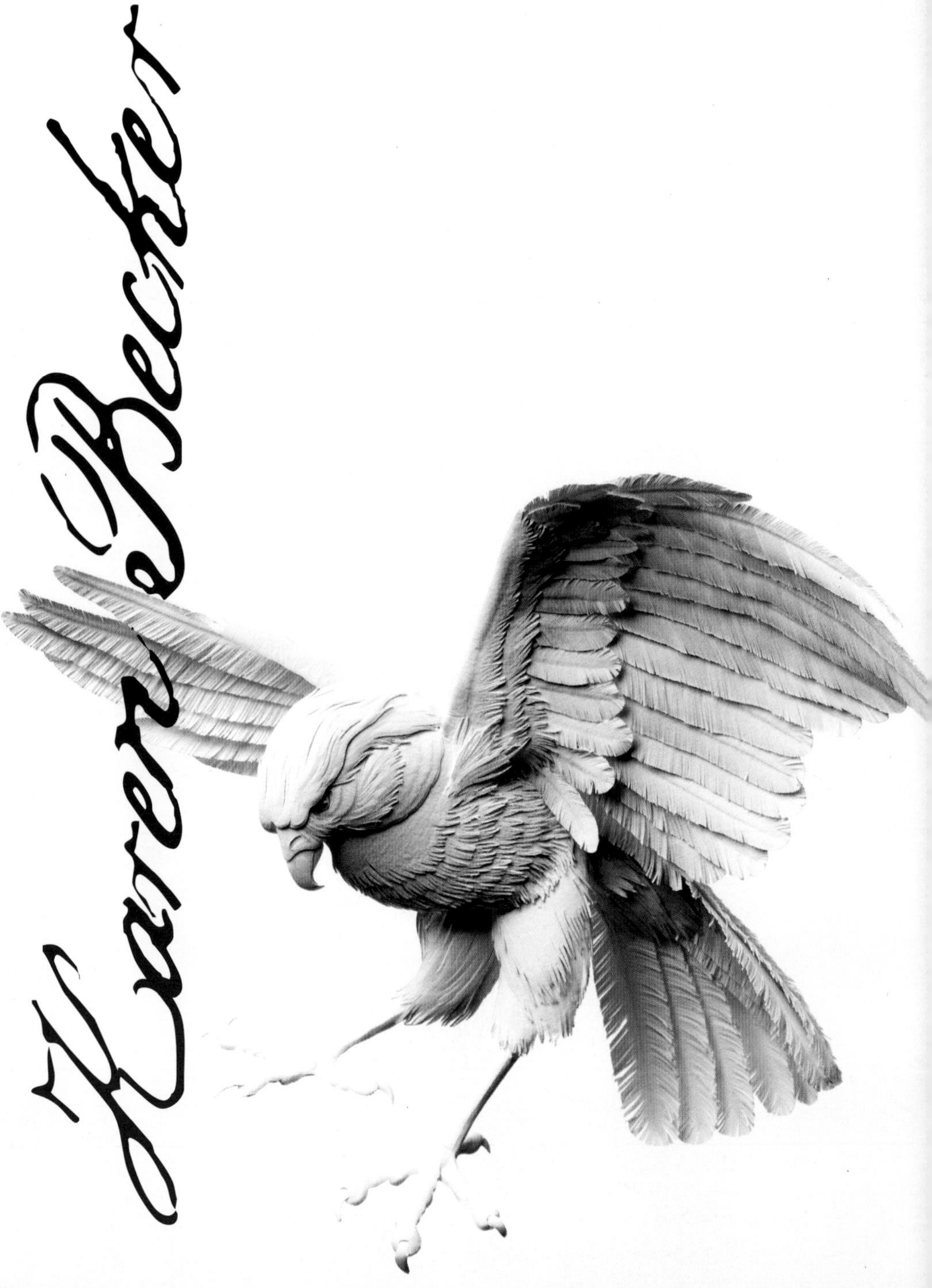
Karen Becker

What animal or environmental issue gets you out of bed, and why? Sustainability and our shrinking and contaminated wild spaces. Wild animals need their own untouched and healthy space in which to exist and thrive. The more resources *we* use the less space and more contaminated resources we leave for the rest of the Animal Kingdom, with whom we share our planet. Ultimately, our ravenous and insatiable appetite for more means our tired, toxic, and worn-out Earth will become unsustainable

What are you doing about it? I'm a veterinarian and a federally licensed wildlife rehabilitator. I give orphaned, injured, and sick wild animals a second chance at life. I work with earth-conscious landowners to establish "safe spots" so that rehabilitated wildlife can be released with a better chance of survival. There are fewer and fewer healthy and safe places for a successful release. Finding people committed to keeping their property free from pesticides, herbicides, sport hunting, development, and industrialized agriculture is challenging—this is true for the homeowner in the suburbs as well as the rancher on 4000 acres. The keys are cooperation and education. I am passionate about environmental education, working together to help people realize the importance of preserving what we have. My hope is that once people are aware of the magnificent natural life all around us, they will want to protect it.

What can everyone do about it? Use the knowledge and compassion you have to help! We should all recycle our waste, pickup after ourselves (don't litter) and learn to co-exist with weeds in your yard. Once you learn that they detoxify the soil, you'll learn to love them, like I do. If you eat meat, choose animals that have been ethically raised and slaughtered. Choose food that is free from chemicals and genetic modification. Commit to a chemical-free yard, home, water and air supply. We should learn to live with less and still be happy, appreciate untouched areas of land and water, and respect the unexplored Respect other's rights—especially if you see a sign posted "Do not enter" or "No respassing." And when a creature needs help, stop and help.

KAREN SHAW BECKER *is a small and exotic animal veterinarian and a U.S. Fish and Wildlife Service licensed wildlife rehabilitator. She is founder of the nonprofit organization, Covenant Wildlife Rehabilitation. Dr. Becker is passionate about species-appropriate nutrition and holistic veterinary medicine, a treatment approach she applies to every patient she sees*

Marc Bekoff

What animal or environmental issue gets you out of bed, and why? Animal abuse keeps me awake at night and gets me out of bed very early in the morning. While I've long been concerned about a wide range of animal abuse, my latest interests are in the growing field of compassionate conservation, a focus on the well-being of individual animals, and the various ways in which humans can rewild themselves and become re-enchanted and reconnected with nature.

What are you doing about it? I want to end to all forms of animal abuse and I spread the word any way I can. I write extensively about animal sentience and abuse. I travel all over the world giving talks and holding workshops, and work with youngsters, inmates, and senior citizens as part of Jane Goodall's Roots & Shoots program. Animals need our help and every individual matters. We don't have to do huge things to make the lives of other animals better and more dignified, we just need to pay attention to how we live and set an example for others, especially youngsters.

What can everyone do about it? In my book, *Rewilding Our Hearts: Building Pathways of Compassion and Coexistence,* I show how simple it is for people to do something for other animals and their homes. We need to stop eating other animals, wearing them, using them for brutal research and educational projects, and using them for entertainment. We need to call attention to animal abuse gently but firmly. In *Rewilding Our Hearts,* I write about what I call "the eight P's of rewilding": being proactive, positive, persistent, patient, peaceful, practical, powerful, and passionate. I've recently added two more, namely being playful and present.

MARC BEKOFF, PhD, is professor emeritus of ecology and evolutionary biology at the University of Colorado, Boulder. A renowned leader in the field of animal behavior, Marc is a fellow of the Animal Behavior Society, a Guggenheim Fellow, and co-founder with Jane Goodall of the Ethologists for the Ethical Treatment of Animals: Citizens for Responsible Animal Behavior Studies. He has published 30 books including The Emotional Lives of Animals, Wild Justice: The Moral Lives of Animals *(with Jessica Pierce),* The Ten Trusts *(with Jane Goodall),* Ignoring Nature No More: The Case for Compassionate Conservation, *and* Rewilding Our Hearts: Building Pathways of Compassion and Coexistence.

Emanuele Biggi

What animal or environmental issue gets you out of bed, and why? I have always had a passion for smaller predators—frogs, toads and salamanders. These amazing animals are so poorly understood that I sometimes think we're still in the medieval era in terms of knowledge and conservation. We're facing a huge amphibian extinction and although some of it is a function of nature itself, the more significant impact is due to improper land use by humans.

What are you doing about it? My conservation work evolved over time. I began as a herpetologist with an interest in communication. I always tried to share my knowledge during science festivals, articles and so on, and photography helped me give an "image" to the concept. I now host a live three-hour daily TV program on nature and the environment in Italy. I collaborate with researchers to photograph their works and to help people know about their studies. I have a strong belief that science must try to be more popular (and that doesn't means "easy and stupid"), so I also organize and manage many scientific expositions with the aim of making the smaller animals more appreciated by the general public. My work always aims to raise awareness and knowledge about the small-sized world on which we all depend.

What can everyone do about it? This is a very large topic, so a narrow answer is impossible. We all, editors and magazines included, should try to only use recycled or responsibly cut wood. Our forests are so important. We should avoid disturbing and killing every animal we think is "disgusting." If people will start to just say, "Oh look, that's a cool toad/spider/frog/snake . . ." without a sign of disgust on their face, maybe the young generations will start to really appreciate ALL the fauna and not just the Disney-like cuddly ones. We must change our minds. Our survival as a species depends on the welfare of many others on the planet Earth.

EMANUELE BIGGI, PhD., focuses on "microcosm" animals, conservation of nature, and science-at-work photography. His work (both articles and pictures) has been published in various publications and magazines from around the world. Besides hosting GEO, an Italian TV program about nature and the environment, he is the scientific advisor for Italian parks and nature reserves, an author and lecturer, curator of scientific expositions, and winner of various international photography prizes.

Frances Bodkin

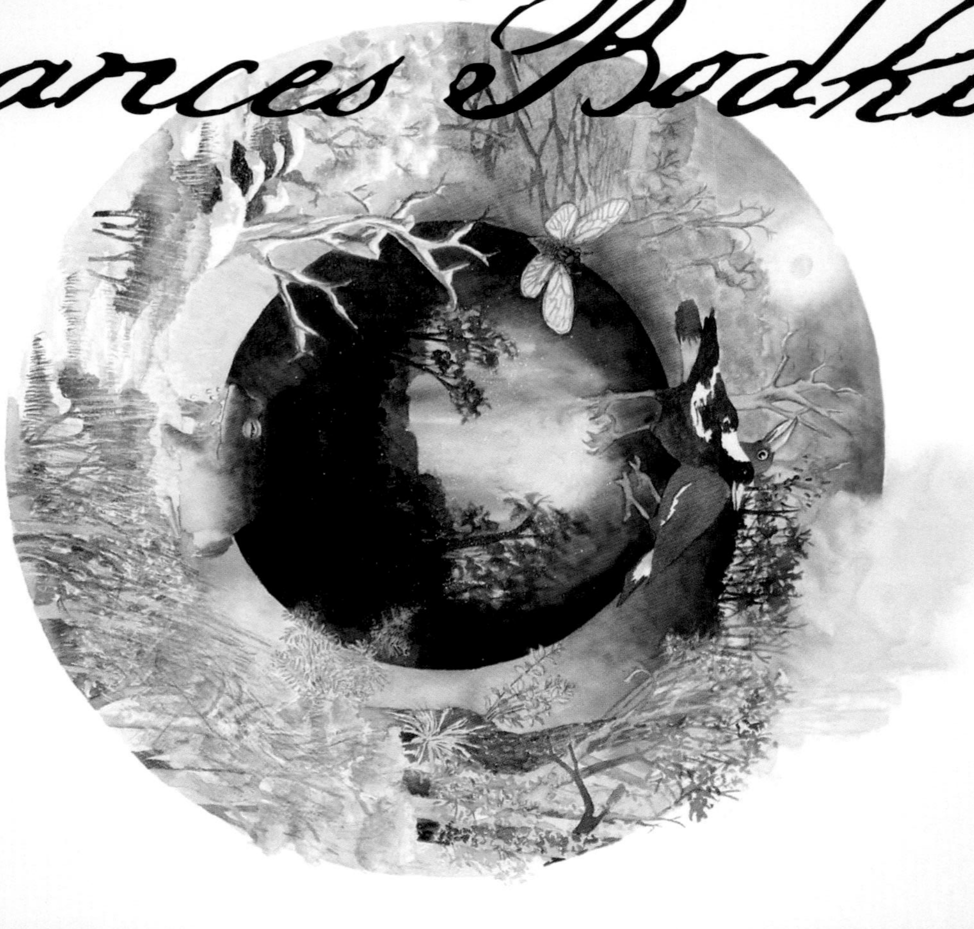

What animal or environmental issue gets you out of bed, and why? The selfishness of humans. The damage we have done to the environment during our short time on this Earth is irreversible. We are fully aware of what we are doing, yet we continue to destroy in the search for ease, wealth and to satisfy our greed. From the child who drops a lollipop wrapper on the ground to the obscenely wealthy miners destroying innumerable habitats and digging great holes in the ground that also destroy the ground water flow for our rivers and waterways, too many of us are guilty.

What are you doing about it? Our children will guide humanity along the pathways of the future, therefore I go to schools within the Aboriginal D'harawal traditional lands and teach the children the beauty of our culture and its respect and love of the land and of the Mother Earth through story and observation. Children have an innate curiosity, it is our duty to awaken that curiosity so that they can observe and enjoy the natural beauty of our lands and environment and the importance of protecting them from the predation of greed.

What can everyone do about it? We must open our eyes to the beauty of the Earth, from the tiniest creature to the largest. Learn how to live without greed. Learn to accept what the earth offers, learn that we do not need to take, that we have all that we need—not necessarily all that we want—to survive and to live happily and simply and to learn from nature.

FRANCES BODKIN I am proudly a woman of the Bidigal clan of the D'harawal Peoples.
At school I was always in trouble for staring out the windows at the clouds and the trees,
the birds and insects and I quickly learned that if I laughed at the wrong time, sang out of tune,
or dropped my slate and pencils with a clatter on the floor, I would be sent outside to sit in
the playground to contemplate my clumsiness. I learned more during those times
contemplating the clouds, or the ants' nests, or even the insects that lived under
the bark of the trees that lined the schoolyards of the various schools that I attended.

What animal or environmental issue gets you out of bed, and why? It's no one animal or environmental issue. We live in an interconnected world and should see the challenges we all face as part of a larger opportunity to create a better, healthier, happier society. There are so many species in peril and there's so much of the environment in danger that a coordinated effort is essential. The Global Goals provides an excellent model: it's a set of 17 commitments to achieve three extraordinary things in the next 15 years: end extreme poverty, fight inequality and injustice, and fix climate change.

What are you doing about it? It's not up to individuals, governments, and non-profit organizations alone to take action—business must stand up to the challenge. Business can—and should be—a force for good. This is our purpose at Virgin, and the reason for which Virgin Unite, our non-profit foundation, exists. We have incubated the B Team to create a plan for all businesses to put emphasis on purpose alongside profit; Ocean Unite to drive ocean conservation and the creation of new marine reserves; the Carbon War Room to reduce climate change at scale; the Branson Centre of Entrepreneurship to nurture the creative minds of tomorrow; and The Elders to work on conflict resolution and tackle climate change.

What can everyone do about it? Hitting the aggressive targets laid out in the Global Goals could change the world for all people, species, and the environment. But if the Goals are going to work, everyone needs to know about them. Tell everyone you can about them, choose your own individual Goal to concentrate on and take action in your community to spread the word. Every individual can focus upon a local issue. Small businesses can concentrate on citywide causes, larger companies on national issues, and international businesses on global causes.

SIR RICHARD BRANSON is Founder of the Virgin Group. Virgin is one of the world's most irresistible brands, with more than 100 companies worldwide and approximately 60,000 employees in over 50 countries. Branson has challenged himself with many record-breaking adventures—from balloon flights to ocean crossings—and described Virgin Galactic as being "the greatest adventure of all." Since starting youth culture magazine Student *at age 16, Branson has found entrepreneurial ways to provoke positive change in the world. In 2004 he established Virgin Unite, the non-profit foundation of the Virgin Group, which strives to make business a force for good.*

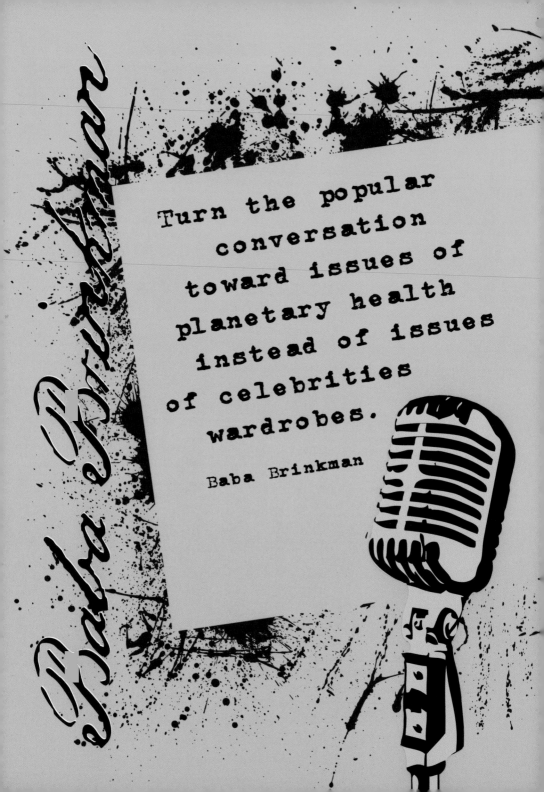

Turn the popular
conversation
toward issues of
planetary health
instead of issues
of celebrities
wardrobes.

Baba Brinkman

What animal or environmental issue gets you out of bed, and why?
Misunderstanding our evolutionary history and our relationship with other living things can lead to all kinds of alienation and entitlement, and the destruction of the environment follows directly from that misunderstanding. I think people would have a different attitude toward extinction and habitat loss if they could see where our species came from and how interdependent we are with other species and with the rest of life. Telling *that* story is one of my principle passions.

What are you doing about it? Mostly, I speak out by writing songs, making videos, and producing music, theater, and comedy shows that help educate the public about biology and psychology and climate change and the importance of biodiversity. The challenge is to make the experience fun and at the same time informative and thought provoking, communicating enthusiasm as well as ideas. Rap music is a useful tool in my campaign.

What can everyone do about it? Read a book about biology, talk to your friends about the ideas in it, identify scientists and conservationists who inspire you, and help to make them better known. If we can turn the popular conversation toward issues of planetary health instead of issues of celebrities' wardrobes, that will be a huge step towards solving the problems at hand. Add your voice to that conversation.

BABA BRINKMAN is a Canadian rap artist and playwright. He is best known for his "Rap Guide" album series, which includes guides to evolution, religion, wilderness, medicine, and his most recent "Rap Guide to Climate Chaos." His work combines hip-hop with comedy, theatre, and big ideas, and has won several awards and award nominations for outstanding writing and performance. He has opened for the likes of Stephen Hawking and Richard Dawkins, and would much rather be a supporting act for rock-star scientists than regular old rock stars.

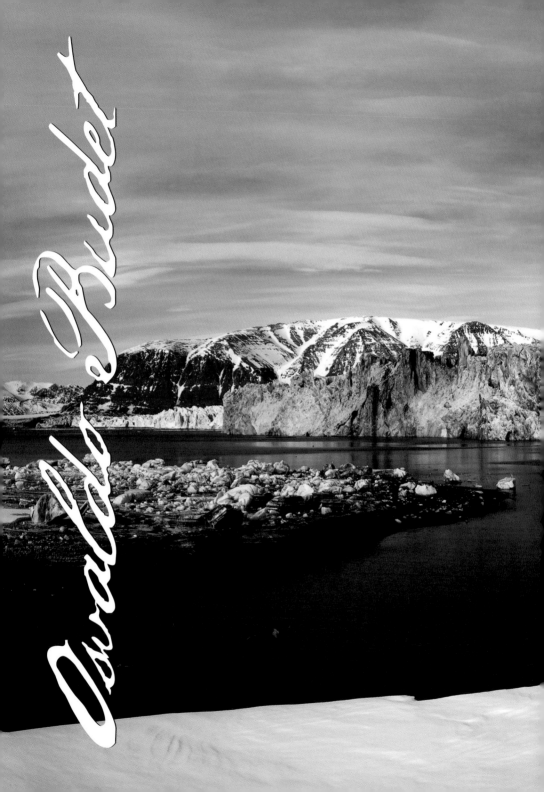

What animal or environmental issue gets you out of bed, and why? Fighting for a better tomorrow inspires my life. Coming from Puerto Rico, an actual colony, drives my work as an artist. In the past, Latin American politics mostly informed my art practice. Now though, I see anthropogenic climate change as the single greatest colonizing force ever witnessed and it is this issue that I am focusing my work around.

What are you doing about it? I create art that explores human impacts on the environment. I want to challenge the relationship we have with politics and the environment. I use film, photography, and painting to portray how our species is markedly changing the planet. I am a member of a political puppeteer performance group working with social issues on and off the island of Puerto Rico. I have been documenting the international scientific community's work in the Arctic and I am working on an exhibition about anthropogenic climate change. I work to link this world issue to local issues here in Puerto Rico.

What can everyone do about it? Climate change is not up for debate—it's irrelevant if you believe it or not. The problem of climate change is beyond individual action. We must work together and be aware of the way we approach and use our global resources. Empirical science points clearly to the direction we are headed in in the business-as-usual scenario, but we are the generation that can change the course of history and get off fossil fuels. Our leaders and corporations must be held accountable. Protest, march, and take to the streets. I am optimistic that we have the tools and know how, we only need to summon the will collectively.

OSVALDO BUDET *is currently a professor of painting at the University Escuela Artes Plastica, San Juan, Puerto Rico. He has worked extensively with communities for social change in Puerto Rico, the U.S., and Germany.*

When I
save a dog
I've changed
its life.

Victoria Burrows

Victoria Burrows

What animal or environmental issue gets you out of bed, and why? Animal rescue gets me up and going at almost any hour of the day. When I get a picture of a dog in distress or abused I go into immediate how-do-I-rescue-or-fix-this mode. Because dogs are the victims so often, I know that if I don't take action right away, a dog may not get an opportunity for a normal and better life. I am euphoric when we can find the best human match for a dog's needs—and know that as move out of their lives, a dog is taken care of for the rest of its life.

What are you doing about it? I started helping with animal adoptions and fostering rescue dogs while casting feature films and television shows. It was so rewarding to come home and see the happy loving faces that appreciated me without question that I founded Star Paws Rescue, a not-for-profit dedicated to helping dogs and cats. I used the name STAR because it represents my film world and the furry critters become my stars and I cast them into the right home. I take care of medical dogs, abandoned dogs and owner-dumped dogs. It's a way to give back. I network dogs to other reputable rescue organizations and always make choices based on what's best for the dog. It's a fulfilling feeling, knowing that when I save a dog I've changed its life. That's awesome angel work here on earth!

What can everyone do about it? If everyone would care for his or her pet as the living, feeling soul that it is, the world would be a better place. If a person owns a dog, it deserves an education just like children do—and the parents/owners need to be trained too. Their stories are many. A woman driving on the freeway saved six-week-old Evita. She saw the pup in the emergency lane and stopped to pick her up. Evita's a happy adult now. If a person sees an animal in distress, make a conscious choice to help.

VICTORIA BURROWS has been in the entertainment industry for more than 30 years. Victoria's huge casting successes include Flight *with Denzel Washington,* Contact *with Jodie Foster,* Cast Away *with Tom Hanks,* Lord of the Rings*, and* 21 Jump Street *to name only a few. To this casting director, who makes her living from the world of make believe, there is no greater success or role more real or dear to*

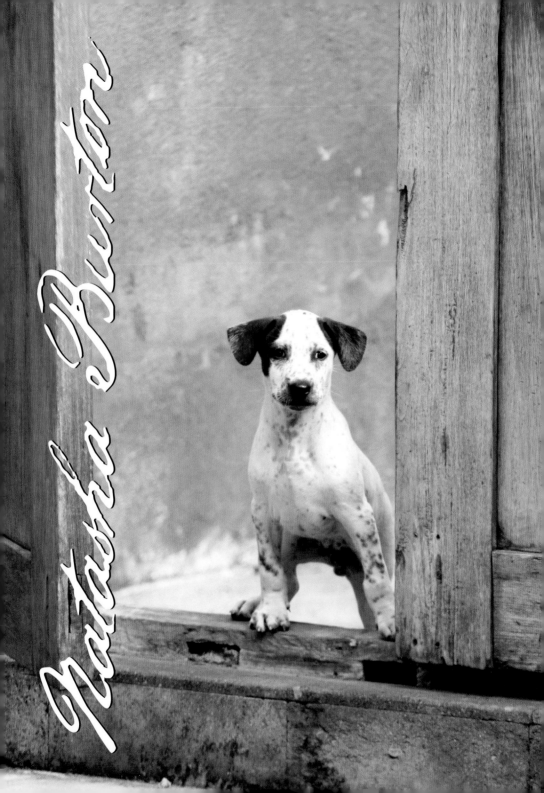

Natasha Bwrton

What animal or environmental issue gets you out of bed, and why? I am passionate about animals, particularly dogs. I'm a nurturer, a feeder, and nothing pleases me more than the sight of happy, healthy animals. I've spent a lot of time in Bali and was always distressed at the plight of the hungry and injured strays. I've spent hours running around trying to feed them, knowing that my small offerings didn't amount to much. I had an overwhelming urge to do something—anything—to help them. We waste so much food and I'm passionate about that too. I don't throw anything out. It goes to the dogs, to the seagulls or if it's compost, it goes back to the earth.

What are you doing about it? In 1999, my friend Paula Hodgson and I started The Bali Street Dog Fund in Australia. Our aim was to raise funds to treat, feed and spay or neuter stray dogs in Bali. Some people thought we were mad. But instead of thinking "Why are we doing this?" we thought, "How can we NOT?" With the help of volunteer and local vets and a handful of caring ex-pats, we got the charity up and running. Within months, we had makeshift mobile clinics, which went from village to village treating and de-sexing strays. Our motto was, "Healing not killing." Because of donations from our amazing supporters, we were able to buy two ambulances, which offer twenty-four-hour emergency vet care. We embarked on education programs in schools and villages to show people how to care for their dogs. It takes just a small amount of care and kindness to turn a frightened, almost-wild stray into a sweet and gentle dog. To date more than 60,000 dogs have been treated and de-sexed.

What can everyone do about it? Don't turn a blind eye. Everyone can make a difference. Donate, buy food or medicines, spread the word, or feed a starving dog (that meal might save its life). And never waste food—someone or something will be grateful for it.

NATASHA BURTON is the original founder of The Bali Street Dog Fund, Australia. She currently lives in Bondi Beach, Sydney. She is an avid animal lover and champions of animal rights. Apart from animals, her great love is snorkeling and the ocean. She spends two months a year in Bali with her rescued street dogs Macan ("Tiger") and Minggu ("Sunday"), who also have Balinese families.

Jonah Cameron

What animal or environmental issue gets you out of bed, and why? Orangutans and their forest homes. Both are being destroyed by palm oil plantations and greedy people. And it's not just the orangutans—amazing animals such as pangolins, apes, monkeys, tigers and really cool insects are just a few of the many animals who are being killed by palm oil plantations every day. We should be protecting animals and plants in the forest, not destroying them for money.

What are you doing about it? I am raising $10,000 for the Borneo Orangutan Survival Foundation to help release an orangutan back into a safe forest. I have a market stall and I sell donated items to raise funds. I also use my stall to raise awareness about orangutans and palm oil. I have a Facebook page, Jonah's Forest Friends, and a lemonade stall, which I use to raise funds.

What can everyone do about it? You can help a lot by only buying products without palm oil in them. Check labels for ingredients, write to companies who are still using palm oil and ask them to stop, and donate money to help people who are working to save animals and forests every day. Spread the word by talking about palm oil. For example, students can check their school canteens and make sure they are palm-oil free, do a project for school about this issue, and have fundraisers for people saving orangutans and the forest.

JONAH CAMERON is a 10-year-old homeschool student, administrator of Jonah's Forest Friends Facebook page, head Junior Animal Carer at Storybook Farm – Sacred Animal Garden, and animal rescuer. He is CEO of both The Market Stall and Lemonade Stand, geologist of the future, inventor of cool stuff, martial arts student, cook, and an orangutan's best friend.

What animal or environmental issue gets you out of bed, and why? The crisis of biodiversity, the rapacious extinction of species due to overexploitation and additional plagues related to human appropriation of Nature, the woeful ignorance with which humanity deals with the occurrence of such a crisis, hoping that techno-solutions will come to the rescue, while they are often turned into techno-nightmares. The crisis is unprecedented. Natural selection never eliminated thousands of irreplaceable species as human greed and utilitarian selfishness are doing now. The value system that has brought about this crisis is unacceptable and must be replaced.

What are you doing about it? The crisis is first one of language and values within the conservation movement. I work to convince my colleagues to avoid using language that refers to wildlife as 'natural capital' and to ecological function as 'ecosystem service.' Unrelenting overuse is not just a challenge for development, it is morally wrong. We are what we speak! We understand what language allows us to understand. The language used to think about the crisis of extinction is part of the problem. It thwarts our ability to understand the essence of losing the irreplaceable when life is at stake. We need to revolutionize the value system that involves Nature, starting with the language. We need a paradigm shift that prioritizes the diversity of life above ANY utilitarian value. Essential human needs must be satisfied by more egalitarian societies, better distribution of wealth and careful production and consumption. Biodiversity cannot take the blame.

What can everyone do about it? Be aware that any practical solution will not suffice if we continue to prioritize our needs above Nature's (all other species and needs), and force Nature to earn its right for existence. It is time to overcome self-deception. While the international community states that poverty has to be alleviated, fisheries discard 40% of what is caught each year because it is cost effective. It's time to stop and redefine good and bad.

CLAUDIO CAMPAGNA is a scientist at the Wildlife Conservation Society (WCS).
His field work was conducted in Patagonia on marine mammals and he continues
to work to create open ocean marine protected areas. Claudio publishes widely
in both scientific and popular literature, and has served on several national,
regional, and international marine conservation committees and specialist groups,
such as the IUCN Species Survival Commission. Claudio is interested in the
philosophy of language applied to the environmental discourse.

What animal or environmental issue gets you out of bed, and why? Researchers estimate that between three and four million pets are euthanized each year in the United States due to pet overpopulation. Irresponsible pet owners—those who allow their pets to breed indiscriminately or abandon their pets because they can no longer keep them or want them—are at the foundation of this alarming statistic.

What are you doing about it? I am an ambassador for One Picture Saves a Life, a campaign that inspires, empowers, and educates animal ambassadors around the world to improve the image of animal rescue and adoption through positive photography and grooming. The goal is to encourage people to adopt pets at their local shelter or rescue as opposed to buying from a breeder or puppy mill. At the same time, we hope to remind everyone that pets are not disposable objects. They are loving members of our family that we must care for and protect.

What can everyone do about it? There are several things people can do to help. Everyone should spay or neuter their pets and encourage family and friends to do the same. When considering bringing a pet into your life, first decide if you are ready for this serious commitment. If you are, please adopt your pet from the local animal shelter or rescue group. You will be not only gaining a new best friend, but also saving a life. You will also discover countless volunteer opportunities in your community to help pets. Even just a few hours a week can result in lives saved. In the past decade, we as a society have come a long way in resolving the pet overpopulation issue, but we still have so much work to do. Thanks to you all for doing anything you can to help.

SETH CASTEEL is an award-winning photographer and established member of the animal rescue community. He is also the New York Times *bestselling author of* Underwater Dogs *and* Underwater Puppies.

Rohan Chhabra

What animal or environmental issue gets you out of bed, and why? The illegal trade of wildlife and an increase in hunting/poaching activities has bought many animal species to the brink of extinction. Animals like the elephant, the rhino, and the tiger are hunted for trophies, ornaments, meat, and the belief in the therapeutic powers of their body parts. This situation, brought about by us, will lead to extinction and will disturb the balance of our planet's ecosystem in ways that nature will not be able to recover from. This haunting scenario affects me as an artist and as a citizen. It gets me out of my bed.

What are you doing about it? I inform and aim to reform. We need to communicate more about this crisis and raise awareness. As a designer, I choose a psychological approach. I've designed a series of hunting jackets that represent the animals under threat and reminds us of our complicity in the problem. The heritage of hunting empowers and may explain why the hunter's jacket has influenced mainstream fashion as a symbol of masculinity and purposefulness. As a fashion item, my hunting jackets empower without guilt, but then remind us of the ultimate source of this potency—the act of slaying a living creature and transforming it into a decorative object, an accessory, a trophy. Rather than condemning the hunter outright, these sculptural garments enable us to recognize the hunter in ourselves. The wearer can experience the symbiotic relationship of hunter and hunted, and perhaps acknowledge the absurdity of this "loop." I work to create quietly disturbing experiences that move from aesthetics to moral reflection.

What can everyone do about it? Be socially informed, relevant, and responsive. When the buying stops, the killing can too. Choose not to consume or use products made from wild animals or the habitat they depend on. Ask what a product is made of and where it comes from. The illegal wildlife trade is a billion-dollar industry and we need to support environmental organizations working to save endangered animals and their habitat. We can make a difference just by our choices. We can move things forward in a considered, skillful, and positive way.

ROHAN CHHABRA'S work has received critical acclaim for its craftsmanship and socially informed, responsive nature. Based in Delhi, India, he holds degrees in fashion and industrial design from Central Saint Martins College of Art and Design in London.

What animal or environmental issue gets you out of bed, and why? Our collective denial and short-term vision when it comes to environmental issues, especially overpopulation, loss of biodiversity, and climate change. As a species, we are currently consuming about 150% of what planet Earth offers. We are eating away and destroying the very planet we depend upon to survive simply to support greedy consumerist systems and unfulfilling life experiences. This mindset has to change.

What are you doing about it? I teach and research design strategies that can lead to better sustainable products and services for the future, and hopefully inspire new generations of designers to be eco-literate and to integrate environmental values into their design propositions for future sustainable manufacturing. I firmly believe that all design education should integrate these essential principles, but unfortunately, it is not yet the case.

What can everyone do about it? Rethink our consumption patterns, from energy to materials and products. Lighten our environmental footprint. We can start with very simple gestures, such as switching off lights when you are not in the room and turning down your thermostat in winter. But also think before you buy, do you really need that new phone, that new jacket? If you do, make sure you invest in products

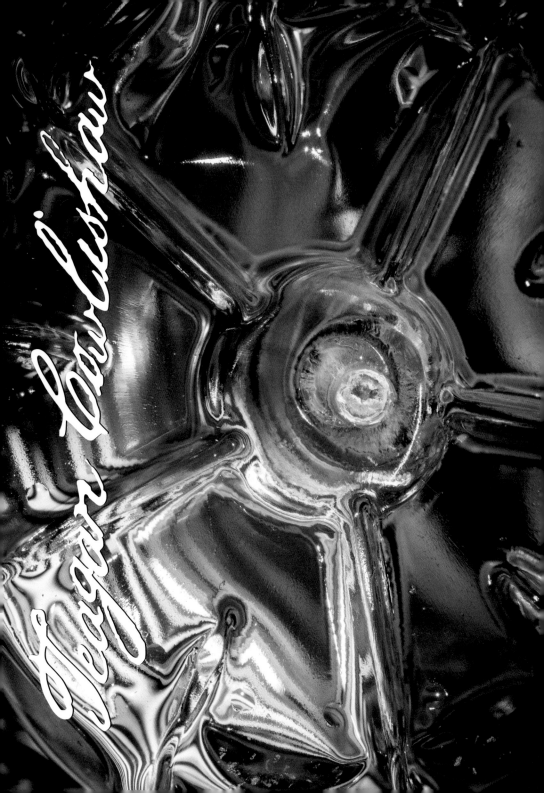

What animal or environmental issue gets you out of bed, and why? Fast fashion," the over-consumption of resources and excessive waste and rubbish. We need to remind ourselves we've only got one Earth, one shot. We need to understand the difference between *needs* and *wants*. We must understand that the actions we take effect many peoples and ecosystems. How do I create mass awareness and have the ability to change human lifestyles dramatically without becoming cynical of our society of consumers?

What are you doing about it? I want to lead by example. I have established a sustainable and ethical fashion label called AARLI that specializes in women's upcycled fashion. AARLI established a dead stock partnership with Nobody Denim in an effort to curb waste and encourage sustainability. It's mutually beneficial for both businesses with all unused products upcycled to extend life span. Our garments are designed and ethically manufactured in Australia. We source sustainable base materials from ethical resources, including sustainable fabrics made from hemp, +PET® (recycled plastic bottles) and upcycle dead-stock denim

What can everyone do about it? Think before you act. Acknowledge that every choice we make directly affects our Earth. Research brands and read labels. Boycott the fast fashion industry and purchase only ethical and sustainable products. Rethink, Reuse, Recycle by shopping for vintage or second-hand clothing and accessories. Minimize landfills by reusing discarded products and upcycling. Take care to extend the life span of products. Launder gently with appropriate products and as needed including:

- consider the energy usage in the aftercare of their garments.
- machine wash in cold water (protected by a pillowcase)
- use alternatives to normal washing powders
- use alternatives to dryers (i.e. air dried, reduce your energy and resource consumption).

TJ COWLISHAW'S kinship lies with the Bardi people (grandmother's ancestry), of the Kimberleys, WA (Family name: Hunter) she is descended from the Chinese pirates of Shanghai (grandfather's ancestry) (Family name: Jan). Teagan's an Indigenous Fashion Designer, Visual Artist + Events Manager from Perth WA. Her Indigenous heritage has led to the naming of her label AARLI (meaning fish in Bardi). AARLI is a sustainable + ethical street wear label that specializes in women's upcycled fashion. An upcycle fashion designer who creates garments from dead stock + offcuts + sustainable material. Through her business, Teagan continues to works with various Indigenous community groups in delivering business and event services.

Theresa L. Markiewicz

What animal or environmental issue gets you out of bed, and why?

Water, water, everywhere,
Nor any drop safe to drink.

Access to clean drinking water is something many of us take for granted, but it is a daily battle for millions of people in Africa, Asia, and parts of Latin America. Contaminated water carries deadly diseases, and 90% of the deaths due to diarrheal diseases, such as cholera and E. coli, are in children under five years old.

What are you doing about it? I work to stop the spread of preventable deaths from water-borne illnesses. I develop new technologies to remove disease-causing microbes from drinking water, including pAge drinking papers, which are antimicrobial paper filters, as seen in *The Drinkable Book™*. The book is both an educational tool and a collection of filters to purify drinking water. We work with the people who need clean water the most, and have conducted field trials in rural communities in northern Ghana, Haiti, Kenya, South Africa, and Bangladesh. WATERisLIFE is one of our partners.

What can everyone do about it? *The Drinkable Book* is just one part of the solution to the water and sanitation crisis. Many water- and health-focused nonprofit organizations need volunteers to get out in the field and to directly help others. Clean water problems are largely found in developing countries, where extreme poverty is also a big issue. Start your own fundraising drive in your local community. Donate to nonprofits already doing work in the field. Write an essay about what clean water means to you. Facilitate a discussion on water issues in your own city. Invite experts in the field to speak at your school. Ultimately, I hope people take the time to learn about these problems and spread awareness to others around them.

THERESA DANKOVICH is a postdoctoral research associate in Civil and Environmental Engineering at Carnegie Mellon University in Pittsburgh, PA, USA. She is also the founder and inventor of pAge drinking paper, which is featured in The Drinkable Book™*.*

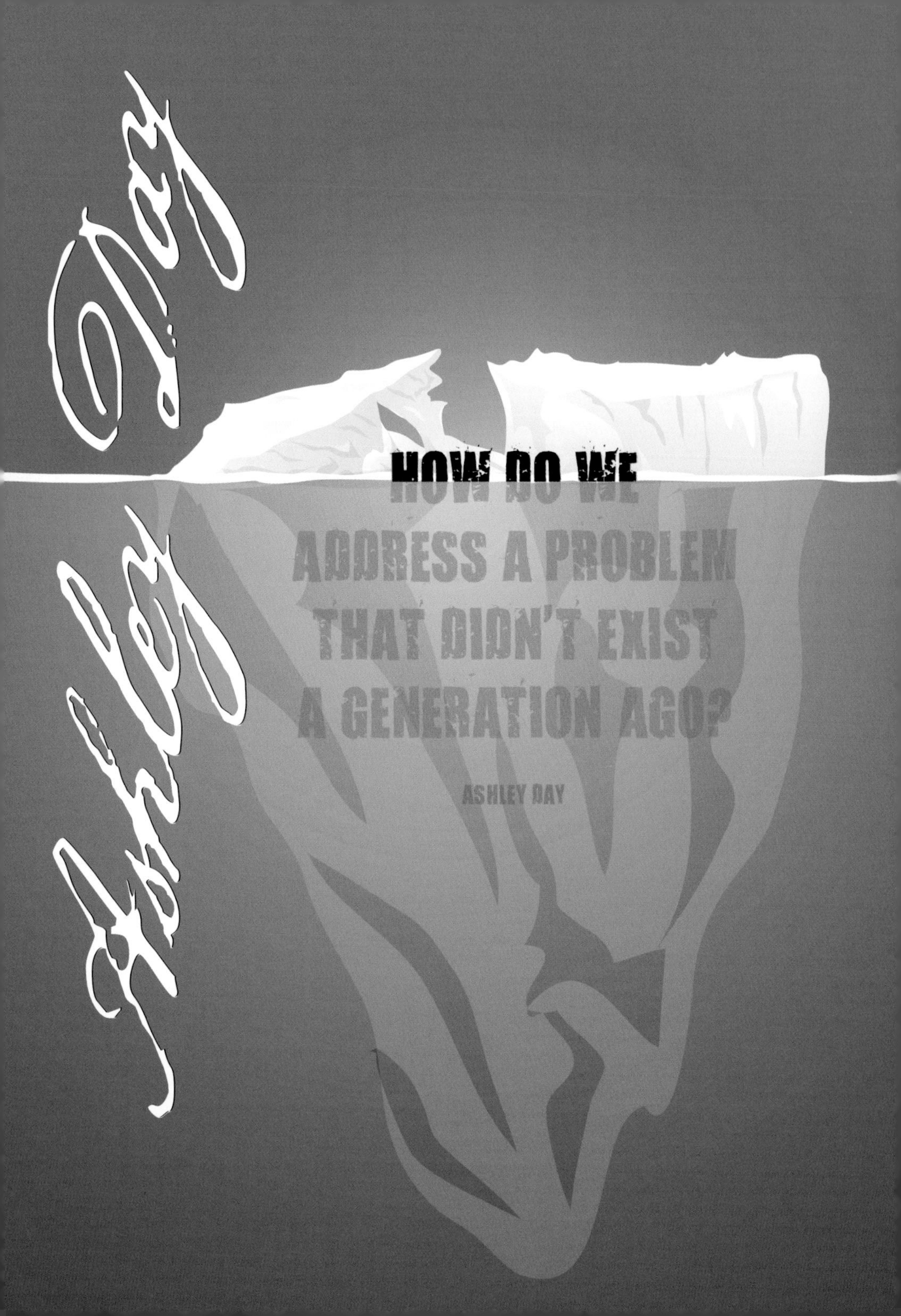
Ashley Day
HOW DO WE
ADDRESS A PROBLEM
THAT DIDN'T EXIST
A GENERATION AGO?
ASHLEY DAY

What animal or environmental issue gets you out of bed, and why? I've always loved the ocean and the majestic feeling I get from observing and playing in "Big Blue." Unfortunately, we are in a global crisis regarding the declining health and pollution of our oceans. The thought that many marine animals may become extinct before our grandchildren are born is simply unbearable. The oceans are our lifeline and essential to the precious balance of nature by which we are all connected. I've been inspired to increase awareness about the human impact on this mysterious and critical component of our planet.

What are you doing about it? How do we address a problem that didn't exist a generation ago? How can business, education, and our environment synergistically move together to benefit one another? As a serial entrepreneur, I've been compelled to develop technologies in which people and industry have the tools needed to create sound business opportunities that simultaneously create social and environmental change. These are foundational tools needed to create a mind shift to preserve our delicate global family tree. I have worked with oil producers decreasing flare-gas pollution (preventing ocean acidification), developed new innovative strategies for safer and cleaner marine environments (oil spill technology), and created a mobile gaming application to educate gamers about marine debris (Future Fighters app) and fund clean-up solutions. I am committed to leaving a lasting legacy for our delicate ecosystem.

What can everyone do about it? WE are the main cause of the problem, but also the key to the solution. Addressing these issues requires responsibility and action at every level. Collaborative efforts of government, businesses, and individuals of all ages can start powerful initiatives to move in the right direction. No person is too small and no company is too large to begin taking action on some level for this movement to take effect. Whether you are a passionate environmentalist, business executive, or avid gamer there is an opportunity for you to make real world change. The most important factor is the desire to get in the game!

ASHLEY DAY attended University of Denver business school and played professional basketball before starting a career as an entrepreneur who develops technologies for sustainable resource recovery and environmental solutions. His gaming app initiative, FutureFighters.org focuses on a new approach to gaming in which people can be educated and involved with global environmental solutions right from the palm of their hands.

Charles Day

THERE ARE CONSEQUENCES TO EVERYTHING WE DO, AND TO THE THINGS WE DON'T.

Charles Day

What animal or environmental issue gets you out of bed, and why? Our planet's future, our husbandry of 8.7 million species, and our own economic destinies are all inextricably linked. Each depends on our ability to build companies that are intentioned and mindful, because I have learned, both as an executive coach to some of the world's most innovative businesses, and as a human being, that there are consequences to everything we do—and to the things we don't. In businesses and in our treatment of animals and the environment I see people make an assumption that hope will suffice in the absence of a vision, that good intentions are a substitute for action. They are not. And they have consequences. Slow to appear in some cases, but consequences as malignant as any cancer when ignored, or worse, when fueled by the belief that the future is always fixable. But the future is fragile, its health as delicate as a butterfly's wing.

What are you doing about it? The future is shaped actively or passively. Passivity is second only to willfulness in its capacity for destruction. The surest path to choosing action is to define your purpose and your company's. Why does your company exist? How is the world improved by its existence? Because, when companies engage in mindful behavior, the world is made healthier, and the ripples roll outward. Google's Purpose is 'organize all the world's data and make it useful.' Every step they take on that journey improves the chances that we will not be masters of our own destruction or that of the 4,000 billion non-human life forms that share this planet with us.

What can everyone do about it? Among Netflix's guiding values is: 'responsible people thrive on freedom and are worthy of freedom.' Imagine the change in our collective behavior if every company believed trust was a viable organizing principle. How might we change our priorities with the self-respect that would result? Our planet needs us to be worthy of trust. So do those with whom we share it. And so, ironically, do our businesses, the vessels capable of carrying future generations to a new world. So, build your business with Purpose and define your values with Humanity. There are consequences. We should be sure they are the ones we mean to leave behind.

CHARLES DAY helps leaders and organizations unlock the economic power of creativity. He is an active board member of PAWS Chicago,

What animal or environmental issue gets you out of bed, and why? The plight of endangered species around the world worries me, but at the moment, what most concerns me is the rate at which elephant and rhino populations are declining due to poaching. Elephant ivory is used purely for aesthetic reasons, and rhinos are being poached out of belief in a myth that the horn works as a cure for cancer and even hangovers (it's utter nonsense, of course). These are the closely watched species; we barely understand the impact of poaching on other species.

What are you doing about it? Through ShadowView Foundation, an organization I co-founded, we're assisting anti-poaching teams throughout Africa and India with drone technology. This technology enables rangers to quickly locate poachers in vast national parks (with much less risk to the rangers themselves). In addition to the anti-poaching work, we're using drones for scientific research into lesser-known species such as dugongs (sea cows), sloth bears, and pangolins. Through a better understanding of these animals, we're able to develop better conservation methods and cooperative partnerships with other conservation organizations.

What can everyone do about it? Support ShadowView (of course)! Practice responsible tourism. Don't buy ivory or get involved in anything that exploits animals. Think about the impact you want to make on the world, and follow your dreams. But if you really want to make an impact right now, right this moment after you read this? Start eating more plant-based, that will make the biggest impact.

*After becoming disillusioned by working in an organized environmental crime unit as a Dutch police officer, **LAURENS** joined the Sea Shepherd Conservation Society. He took part in three anti-whaling campaigns and became a prominent character in the Discovery Channel's "Whale Wars." During an attempt to film seal clubbing in Namibia, he got the idea of using drones for conservation. To this end, he and Steve Roest founded the ShadowView Foundation in 2013. It is one of the first organizations in the world to use drones for wildlife surveillance and to fight against poaching. Laurens was a finalist for the Future for Nature Award in 2014 and 2015 and an ambassador for the Jane Goodall Institute Netherlands.*

Dechen Dorji

We must SAVE
the PRIMAL values
of WILDNESS
in ourselves and
our BEAUTIFUL
planet SO that
the UNBORN
will get to
HEAR the
ROAR.

DECHEN DORJI

What animal or environmental issue gets you out of bed, and why? Protecting our wildlife populations, their habitat, and their beautiful stories of evolution and co-existence gives me a reason to keep getting up and fighting for the rights of the wild and innocent. We must garner the support and goodwill of like-minded souls around the world and continue raising our voice for the voiceless. We must save the primal values of wildness in ourselves and our beautiful planet so that the unborn will get to hear the 'roar,' see the beauty of our jungles and be connected with the past and the future. We must keep that spirit alive, passion burning – in ourselves, in our institutions, in our vision to save the remaining populations of wildlife across the world.

What are you doing about it? In Bhutan, we work with governments, civil society groups, and students to conserve and protect our wildlife. We are using the simple technology of camera trapping to expose the wild wonders of our forests so that young and the old can cherish and appreciate the beauty and values of wildlife. We want a camera trap to be the only trap these animals encounter, taking pictures of them as they pass by.

What can everyone do about it? We all have to play our part, no matter how small. Every effort, every voice, every dollar will count. We must continue to learn to make informed choices and decisions. We must all come together for a zero – poaching future.

DECHEN DORJI is the World Wildlife Fund for Nature country representative for Bhutan. Prior to joining the World Wildlife Fund, he served as a public policy researcher and professional assistant to His Majesty the King. He received a Master of Environmental Management degree from Yale University and an Undergraduate Honors degree in Forestry from University of Wales, UK. Mr. Dorji has worked in remote parts of east Bhutan managing regional forestry and environmental proj He also founded the Ugyen Wangchuck Institute for Conservation and Environment in Bhutan.

Pre-surgery dogs.

What animal or environmental issue gets you out of bed, and why? There are an estimated 300 million street dogs on the planet. In many parts of the world, the street dog population continues to be subject to mass culling campaigns often driven by understandable fears about the risk of transmission of rabies from dogs to humans. However, this cruel approach has been shown to be entirely ineffective at achieving a lasting reduction in street dog numbers or rabies incidence. Thankfully, in an increasing number of countries it's illegal to cull street dogs as a population control measure. If these countries seek assistance to address the welfare of the street dogs and to control their numbers by humane and effective means, it is imperative that animal-welfare organizations offer all possible support.

What are you doing about it? For the last decade, Vets Beyond Borders has been working with Indian governments to establish and operate effective animal birth control and anti-rabies (ABC-AR) campaigns, including clinical training of local veterinary and allied staff; sterilizing and vaccinating street dogs; providing volunteer veterinarians and paraveterinarians to assist with clinical work; developing public education and awareness programs on responsible pet ownership, zoonotic diseases, and attitudes to street dogs; and working with local authorities to address issues such as garbage disposal and pet registration. In areas where ABC-AR is carried out in a well-organized and sustained manner, street dog populations and rabies incidence are reduced. Communities come to understand that a stable population of rabies-vaccinated street dogs acts as a biological buffer against the influx of feral, unvaccinated dogs.

What can everyone do about it? In countries with street dog populations, support those groups involved in well-organized ABC-AR projects. Encourage local authorities to support such work, to develop effective regional or national programs, and to prohibit culling campaigns.

*As a veterinarian, **IAN** has been an animal welfare campaigner since 2004. He has devised and delivered surgical training courses in the Asia-Pacific region, is the author of widely referenced publications on clinical aspects of Animal Birth Control and Anti-Rabies (ABC-AR) projects, and has been a regular guest speaker at animal welfare meetings. Ian was elected inaugural president of Vets Beyond Borders, Australia (VBB). He is a strong proponent of the "one health" philosophy, promoting the collaboration of veterinarians, doctors and other health professionals in efforts to combat disease. Ian operates a neurological and neurosurgical referral practice in Adelaide, South Australia.*

Kelly Dowst

What animal or environmental issue gets you out of bed, and why? Unnecessary waste and mindless consumption. As a species, we do not always tread lightly. People are aware of the impact certain industries and practices have on the planet, but we're all caught up in the business of *want* and economic growth. It is possible to opt out of this sort of lifestyle without becoming a hermit or doomsday prophet.

What are you doing about it? I began scouring flea markets and charity stores for vintage fashion, fabric, and homewares in my early teens and I've been making and reinventing things in my own trial-and-error way since I was a girl. I write about appreciating the used, worn, vintage, and second-hand, and recycling discarded items to extend their life rather than buying new all the time. I also advocate do-it-yourself projects and rediscovering lost skills like sewing, furniture upholstery and knitting—not just for the environment's sake, but for the joy and pleasure to be found in making things by hand. It's about care and seeing the connection we have with the life of objects.

What can everyone do about it? Think about the earth's finite resources and consider ways to consume less. Boycott companies that advocate waste (such as the 'fast fashion' industry) and be inventive. We all need to reduce, reuse, and recycle.

What animal or environmental issue gets you out of bed, and why? Water conservation. Why are we still using drinking water to water our gardens? Our water supply is finite, not endless. It's a difficult fact for those of us living in first-world countries. We're so used to turning on the tap and getting clean, fresh drinking water, but so many people waste water keeping their gardens irrigated. They should be recycling their used water with greywater systems and harvesting rainwater in tanks!

What are you doing about it? I have a greywater system and rainwater-collection tanks in my home. (Greywater is wastewater from baths or showers, bathroom or kitchen basins, and laundry machines.) The irrigation system for watering my garden is hooked up to the greywater system and that system is backed up by the rainwater tanks. All the water that falls on my roof is diverted into my garden. This stops excess runoff in our storm water systems and insures that my runoff doesn't contribute to ocean pollution.

What can everyone do about it? Water conservation should be a natural part of everyday life. Everyone needs to think of water as the precious, life-giving commodity it is. We should be reducing water waste and protecting the clean water we do have. We all can help. Install a rainwater tank and greywater system. Fix leaking taps and toilets. Install water-saving toilets and showerheads. Take quick 4-minute showers. Wash your dishes in a filled sink rather than washing them under a running tap. Turn off the tap while you brush your teeth. Plant native and drought-resistant plant species in your garden. Use a broom instead of a hose to clean driveways and pathways.

*International-award-winning Australian designer and author **JAMIE DURIE, OAM**, is a passionate environmentalist. Durie and his team have received more than 34 international design awards and gold medals in garden design including the Medal of the Order of Australia for services to the environment and design and the Centenary Medal for services to the environment, television, and the community. He has written numerous books about garden design; designs furniture from natural materials that are sustainable; and hosts an environmentally oriented cable and syndicated television series with an audience in the millions.*

Dr. Sylvia Earle

What animal or environmental issue gets you out of bed, and why? The impact that humans have had on our planet in my lifetime is greater than during all preceding human history. As a witness to these changes, I am compelled by what's happened to the sea. Ignorance is the biggest problem of all for the ocean. People don't tend to think about the ocean when they think of what we need to do to take care of the planet—as if the ocean somehow doesn't matter or is so vast that there is nothing that we could possibly do to harm it. But that's not true. The ocean has limits; there is only so much that we can take out before it will be empty of fish and other sea life, and there is also a limit to how much pollution the ocean can absorb before this vital living system will no longer be able to function.

What are you doing about it? I founded Mission Blue/The Sylvia Earle Alliance to inspire people to see for themselves and to use all means at their disposal to spark a movement to create a global network of marine protected areas, "Hope Spots," large enough to save and restore the ocean, the blue heart of the planet. By designating Hope Spots around the world, we are highlighting areas of the ocean in need of special protection with the goal of safeguarding at least 20% of the ocean by 2020.

What can everyone do about it? Look in the mirror, consider your talents, and think about how you might use them to make a difference for the ocean. Some have artistic skills, others are good with numbers or have a way with words. Everyone has power to make a difference as an individual or by joining the company of others who share a common goal. The key is in knowing that what you do matters, including doing nothing!

*National Geographic Society Explorer in Residence **DR. SYLVIA EARLE** has been named a Living Legend by the Library of Congress, first Hero for the Planet by TIME magazine, and 2014 Woman of the Year by Glamour. She's an oceanographer, explorer, author, and lecturer who has led over 100 expeditions and logged over 7,000 hours underwater. Dr. Earle is the subject of the Netflix documentary Mission Blue.*

Rosemary Elliot

There are no qualifications needed. Animals just need our kindness.

Rosemary Elliot

What animal or environmental issue gets you out of bed, and why? What drives me is a passion to raise awareness of animal sentience. If people understand that animals have interests and can experience both suffering and joy, this becomes life changing. Once we have seen an animal as a feeling, thinking being, we then have a moral obligation to notice how that animal is living. Are their needs being fulfilled or are they exposed to cruelty and neglect? Are they able to live according to their nature or are their experiences restricted in the service of human interests? Are they able to enjoy positive mental states or are their lives marred by pain and distress, or at best, tolerance of their existence? Whether these questions are applied to production animals, domestic, wild or 'feral' animals, animals used in entertainment, sport, research, teaching, or human services, we are left with the same ethical issue—once we notice, we cannot forget. The question then becomes, how should we act to improve the lives of the animals who have awakened our compassion?

What are you doing about it? In 2011, my colleagues and I founded Sentient, The Veterinary Institute for Animal Ethics, to provide a voice for veterinarians to play a leading role in the animal protection movement. Sentient is unique in a few important ways. First, being driven by veterinarians, we use science to address animal welfare issues, but do so within an ethical framework, guided by a recognition of animal sentience. Second, we welcome associate members of other professions, which provide a greater richness to our work. Third, we are independent of government and industry, removing the conflict of interest that often prevents veterinarians from advocating more freely for animals. We produce submissions to government and industry, support students, disseminate research, provide veterinary expertise to other organizations, participate on committees, write articles, and present at public and political forums on issues of animal welfare and ethics.

What can everyone do about it? Everyone can improve the lives of animals by simply being aware of them, considering their needs and speaking up when these are not met. There are no qualifications needed. Animals just need our kindness. We can make a difference through our daily actions and choices, including how we treat the animals directly around us, and how we select food and other products.

ROSEMARY ELLIOT is the current president of Sentient. She graduated from the University of Sydney in veterinary science after establishing a career in clinical psychology. Her special interests are animal sentience, the human-animal bond, and the plight of production animals.

Alexis Fasseas

People will rally to help
when they know there is a problem.

Alexis Fasseas

What animal or environmental issue gets you out of bed, and why? As advanced as our society is about animal issues, the killing of homeless pets is still an accepted management tool. The sad reality is that animals are victims of pet overpopulation. People are the cause of the problem, but, more importantly, we are also the solution. How do we bring about mass awareness and unite people in solving this problem?

What are you doing about it? In 1997, the year my mom and I founded PAWS Chicago, more than 42,000 cats and dogs were killed in the city's shelters—even more shocking, no one in Chicago even knew. We started with a single adoption event, bringing homeless dogs and cats to the bustling retail stores on Michigan Avenue and talking about the tragic killing. From that one day, an entire movement came to life in Chicago—all because people will rally to help when they know there is a problem. Since then, we focused our work on engaging people in the cause of homeless animals. When you come from the business world, you are always thinking about leveraging your resources and finding solutions. Our entire organization is built around bringing more and more people into our tent—as volunteers, ambassadors, adopters, fosters, donors, spay/neuter clients, and general animal enthusiasts. PAWS Chicago reaches all sectors of our community, from luxury retailers to our door-to-door outreach efforts in Englewood, the most economically challenged community in Chicago. Animals are a universal human passion. Animal welfare can be the conduit that brings people together. Today PAWS Chicago is one of the largest no-kill animal welfare organizations in the United States. Last year, our volunteer force was the equivalent of 50 full time employees. Euthanasia in our community has fallen by 77% since our first event. Community engagement has fueled this transformation.

What can everyone do about it? Get involved! Spreading the word about pet homelessness and euthanasia is an easy first step. When people find out what pets are facing in a community's sheltering system, they respond. They are mobilized to volunteer, donate, adopt, spay/neuter, and continue spreading the word to their networks. It's through that mobilization that we build no-kill communities..

ALEXIS FASSEAS is formally trained in law and business and received her JD-MBA from Northwestern University School of Law/Kellogg School of Management. Her experience runs the gamut of the business lifecycle, from start-up to growth, restructure, and turnaround. As a volunteer, Alexis co-founded and has helped build PAWS Chicago into one of the nation's largest no-kill humane organizations, overseeing communications, branding, and strategic planning.

What animal or environmental issue gets you out of bed, and why? Earth is our only home. I deeply care and worry about our planet and all its living forms. I cannot pick one specific cause to fight for; they are too many. The state of pollution on land and at sea overwhelms me. The scope of human destruction spread on nature and on all beings torments me. It seems to be an irreversible mourning.

What are you doing about it? I'm rather a pro-activist than an activist. I apply my ethics every day to my immediate environment: my consumption, my waste. I use recycled material in my art—despite its fashionable trend. Instead of purchasing "noble" fine art materials, I use what is available in my daily life, junk mail, fruit stickers, etc. Salvaging reveals the value of the neglected, the obsolete. Obsolescence is an aberration in nature where all is inherently recycled. I scrupulously follow recycling rules; I keep educating myself. Then I teach my child about nature and our direct action to preserve it versus exploiting it. I taught her basic deeds such as turning the faucet and light off and explained to her why we should avoid wasting water and energy. It is considerably efficient. I share with her my fascination with nature. I regularly ask her to choose a cause toward which we make a donation.

What can everyone do about it? Reconnect with nature and its biodiversity. Don't take anything for granted, not even the air you breathe. Encourage scientific research and environmental education. Science can find solutions to mend Earth. For example, The Nobel prize in Physics 2014 (Shuji Nakamura, Isamu Akasaki, and Hiroshi Amano) was awarded "for the invention of efficient blue light-emitting diodes which has enabled bright and energy-saving white light sources." I believe that environmental education should be part of the school curriculum from the earliest age. Let's all be citizens of Earth.

PAULINE GALIANA is a French-born artist living in New York City. She pursued her master of fine arts at ESAG in Paris. Her work is in collections and museums around the world. She uses multiple disciplines, diverse media, and social inputs to focus on actively engaging the viewer in a visual conversation. The concept of poetic narration through visual media runs through her work, as does a reflection on the sources of, and how, one recycles, creative energy.

Peter Gilmore

What animal or environmental issue gets you out of bed, and why? Plants and food. There are thousands of heirloom varieties of fruits and vegetables that have incredible flavors and different textures that we don't really know about—so many great colors and flows and textures. I want a great variety of food options to work with. But seeds will not survive more than a couple of years unless they're re-grown. Some of these incredible varieties are kept alive sometimes by one community or one family. Unless we embrace these varieties—both in produce and proteins—we're going to lose many foods, and with them, diversity and sustainability.

What are you doing about it? I'm a chef. I work to produce original, beautifully crafted food with a big emphasis on layers of texture and flavors to create an overall sense of balance. Food that tastes delicious and looks beautiful takes you on a journey of different sensations and makes you think about where it came from. I work with farmers I know and with fishermen who use simple, sustainable methods. I try to find sources of grass-fed cattle. We all have a responsibility to make sure that animal welfare is looked after and our food is environmentally produced.

What can everyone do about it? Pay attention to where your food comes from. Learn about all the ingredients that are used to produce, package, and manufacture your food. Don't buy genetically modified (GMO) food. Make sustainable choices as often as possible and animal welfare decisions if you're eating meat. Eat more vegetables, eat a greater variety, go to farmers markets, and support smaller producers. Sustain diversity in our food systems. Enjoy food that is grown organically—it's fresher and tastes better. Eat fish that are caught sustainably so your children can also eat fish. Feel good about what you do. It's going to taste delicious.

PETER GILMORE, a native Australian, is the executive chef of Quay restaurant in Sydney. Since 2001, Peter's creative and original cuisine means that Quay is consistently voted one of the top 25 restaurants in the world. He was inspired to cook at a young age and started his apprenticeship at 16. Critical recognition came in 2000 when Peter was the head chef at De Beers Restaurant at Whale Beach. Peter's next step was as head chef at Quay, and he has never looked back. In 2010, Peter released his first cookbook, Quay: Food Inspired by Nature. *Peter is a passionate gardener.*

Dr. Jane Goodall

What animal or environmental issue gets you out of bed, and why? Many issues get me out of bed, determined to fight on. Right now, I'm concerned about the slaughter of Africa's elephants and rhinos. Especially elephants. I have spent hours with them. They are long-lived and intensely social, with long-term bonds linking family members. They are highly intelligent and emotional. The thought of elephants killed for their tusks, for ivory ornaments and trinkets sickens me. The thought of rhinos slaughtered for their horns to provide worthless medicinal products, appalls me.

What are you doing about it? The Jane Goodall Institute supports campaigns to raise awareness about the suffering of the animals. Too many people think elephants "shed their tusks," or that ivory comes from animals who have died a natural death. We provide information to let them know about the truth and the horrific suffering. I have been interviewed for at least five documentaries that explain the situation. And, through our Roots & Shoots program, young people are creating their own campaigns that expose the shocking cruelty and suffering of elephants and rhinos.

What can everyone do about it? First and foremost, DO NOT BUY IVORY. Share information about the cruelty in social media. Join the various campaigns and marches, donate money if you can to support the rangers, or support any of the other groups that are working desperately to raise awareness and funds to slow the killing.

DR. JANE GOODALL DBE, is an English primatologist, conservationist, and UN Messenger of Peace. Considered the world's foremost expert on chimpanzees, Jane is best known for her study of wild chimpanzees in Tanzania that has spanned more than five decades. Jane is the founder of the Jane Goodall Institute and Jane Goodall's Roots & Shoots program and has worked extensively on conservation, humanitarian, and animal welfare issues.

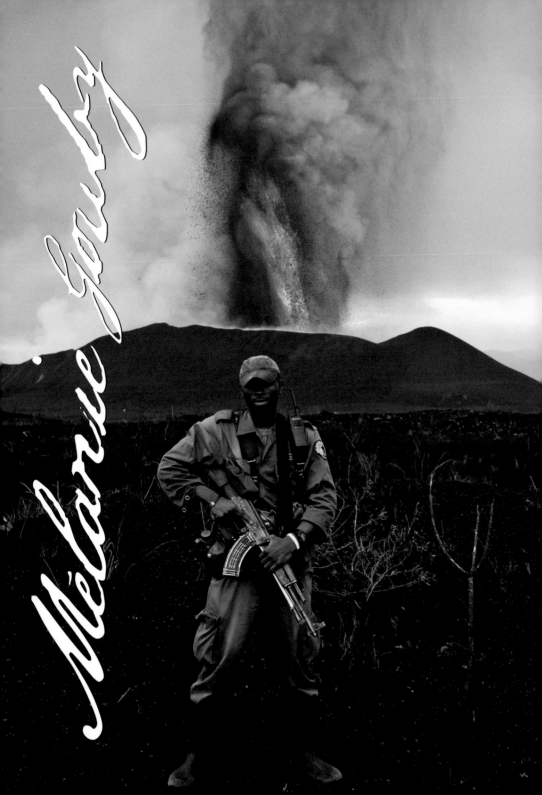

Mélanie Gouby

What animal or environmental issue gets you out of bed, and why? For years, I lived and worked as a journalist in the Democratic Republic of Congo, covering the bloodiest conflict since World War II. The human rights violations, massacres, and mass displacement I witnessed all seemed to be more pressing issues than safeguarding the environment, until I started investigating an oil company prospecting in the Virunga National Park, Africa's oldest and most biodiverse park. It struck me that the people who were trying to appropriate and destroy this protected land were also fueling tensions and conflict, while those who took care of the park had been working for the well-being and the security of all communities around Virunga. Wars already are, and will increasingly be, related to the way we treat our planet and manage its natural resources. That makes stemming climate change and the loss of biodiversity humanity's greatest challenge, but also its greatest opportunity for change.

What are you doing about it? As a journalist, I am an investigator as well as a storyteller. Digging up inconvenient truths and evidence of wrongdoing is not enough if no one pays attention. While investigating the oil company, I met filmmaker Orlando von Einsiedel and we teamed up on his documentary Virunga to denounce the illegal activities of the oil company, but also to highlight the tremendous work of the park rangers who risk their life every day to protect Virunga's diverse wildlife, especially mountain gorillas. The combination of muckraking journalism and the rangers' compelling message of hope has received worldwide attention and brought a great deal of support to the park.

What can everyone do about it? It's important to educate ourselves and become aware of the scale of the environmental crisis we are facing, but also to be excited about all the new opportunities arising. Look for people, charities, and businesses that are doing something positive near you and engage with them. It's not really the planet that needs saving, it is us and we will only succeed by working together. Like nature's complex ecosystems, all environmental issues are interrelated, so every small action, every single person changing her mindset, can make a difference.

MÉLANIE GOUBY is Le Figaro's East Africa correspondent and an investigative journalist focusing on environmental crimes and conflict. Her work is featured in the award-winning documentary Virunga. From 2011 to 2014, she lived in the Democratic Republic of Congo where she covered the M23 rebellion for The Associated Press.

Temple Grandin

What animal or environmental issue gets you out of bed, and why? When I started my career in the early 1970s, many people were extremely abusive to cattle, especially when administering vaccinations, transporting, or slaughtering them. Over the years, I helped improve handling practices and taught people to use gentler methods and better equipment. We now face a new problem that I call "biological system overload." This occurs when pets or food animals become dysfunctional and suffer due to an overemphasis on genetic manipulation for either appearance or production traits—bulldogs have been so highly bred that they have become deformed freaks who have difficulty breathing and dairy cows bred for milk production become lame, have a shortened life, and end up skinny, emaciated bone racks. Both the bulldog and the dairy cow have chronic conditions that cause long-term suffering. Laying hens suffer from biological system overload, too. Many older laying hens have broken bones due to osteoporosis because they have been bred to lay too many eggs. This problem may endanger the food supply because the same principles also apply to plants. Energy is required for a plant or animal to produce food. If all of its resources are put into producing food, then there may be fewer resources for disease resistance.

What are you doing about it? Some people may decide to stop eating animal products. I have made the choice to continue to eat animal protein because my metabolism requires it. The animals that are raised for meat, milk, or eggs should be bred for optimal production and not maximum. The animals must have a decent life that is worth living. I give many lectures to veterinary and animal science students and introduce the concept of biological system overload.

What can everyone do about it? People who can afford it should buy animal products from specialty markets that have high standards for both animal welfare and sustainability, support local agriculture, and never buy pets that have functional defects due to breeding. In the developing world, the first step is to stop the worst of the suffering and reduce biological system overload and overt abuse.

TEMPLE GRANDIN is a professor of animal science at Colorado State University. She has written and edited many books, an HBO movie has been made about her life, and she has received many awards from both agricultural and animal advocacy organizations.

Rodney Walsh

What animal or environmental issue gets you out of bed, and why? That's easy! Two things: the dangers of misinformation about pet food, and my dogs, because it's probably time for a walk. Pet owners today are bombarded with confusing and inaccurate information about feeding their pets. Breeders, shelters, trainers, conventional/holistic/integrative veterinarians, manufacturers and even well-meaning friends all want to give their two cents' worth. (The worst part is that most pet owners believe that they are doing the very best thing when it comes to feeding their pet.) Following the wrong advice can either tragically shorten or end the lives of our companion animals. I know. I followed the marketing claims of a manufacturer and the food I fed two of my beloved pets ended up destroying their digestive systems. I didn't research the food properly. I don't want any other pet owner to experience the same ache.

What are you doing about it? I'm honoring the vow I made to my pets by building the largest virtual megaphone EVER and, through media, lectures and social media, I shout out loud to my fellow pet parents around the world. I want to help expose every loophole that pet food manufacturers can find. With almost 1,000 blog posts and magazine articles written so far, I use photos to help communicate the ever-so-important message. Each has to be more creative than the next to keep the pet owners' attention. Once I grab their attention, I plant the seed in hopes of it blossoming and inspiring.

What can everyone do about it? Pet guardians must take more responsibility when it comes to the overall health of their pets. People need to take ten minutes out of their busy days and research. An educated, informed, and well-researched community of pet owners can only put more pressure on the pet food industry to be better. When pet owners know better, they will only do better.

RODNEY HABIB is an award-winning blogger, writer, lecturer, teacher, and founder of the award-winning premium pet food Planet Paws who spreads his message through more than 10 million news feeds, and is, more important, a pet parent. Today Rodney stands on the frontline among pet owners who demand a change in the ever-declining world of pet food and hopes to inspire pet owners to ask more of their manufacturers.

What animal or environmental issue gets you out of bed, and why? What gets me up and moving is when I see how wasteful people around the world are with their 'stuff'. People throw everything away, regardless of whether it can be reused or not. This makes me sit up and take notice because the planet only has so many resources. If we continue to throw things away mindlessly, our planet will be trashed. This issue fuels me.

What are you doing about it? I run a non-profit organization and collect used or new denim jeans of any color or condition and shoes and send them to be recycled. The denim I collect is 100% remanufactured into denim housing insulation. The shoes I collect are recycled or redistributed to those in need. My goal is to recycle as many pairs of jeans and shoes as that I can. In total, I have saved more than 27,000 jeans and 15,000 pairs of shoes from the landfill in seven years, drastically reducing the amount of waste in local landfills. I also advocate what I do: even if someone cannot donate, they can spread the word about recycling.

What can everyone do about it? The great thing about recycling is that it's pretty easy to do. Everyone can recycle something. I am only one person and my actions have impacted my community and region of the U.S. greatly. If everyone made one small change, for example recycling cans and bottles instead of throwing them away, it will make a large impact. That's what I love about recycling, it's easy to do, anyone can do it and it helps keep our planet beautiful.

*In 2009, at age 8, **EREK** read an article in his favorite magazine that sparked his interest in recycling denim jeans. That article led him to take action and has resulted in the collection of over 27,000 pieces denim that were repurposed and kept out of landfills. The denim collected over seven years translates into enough material to insulate over 54 homes with UltraTouch™ Denim insulation. In 2011 at age 10, Erek added shoes to his recycling mission and has kept over 15,000 pairs of shoes out of the landfill. By holding recycling drives, he hopes to spread awareness of the ability to recycle items that may otherwise get thrown away. Through his non-profit, GoGreen Ohio, 15-year-old Erek arranges collection drives, public drop-off sites, speaks to students, and advocates the benefits of recycling.*

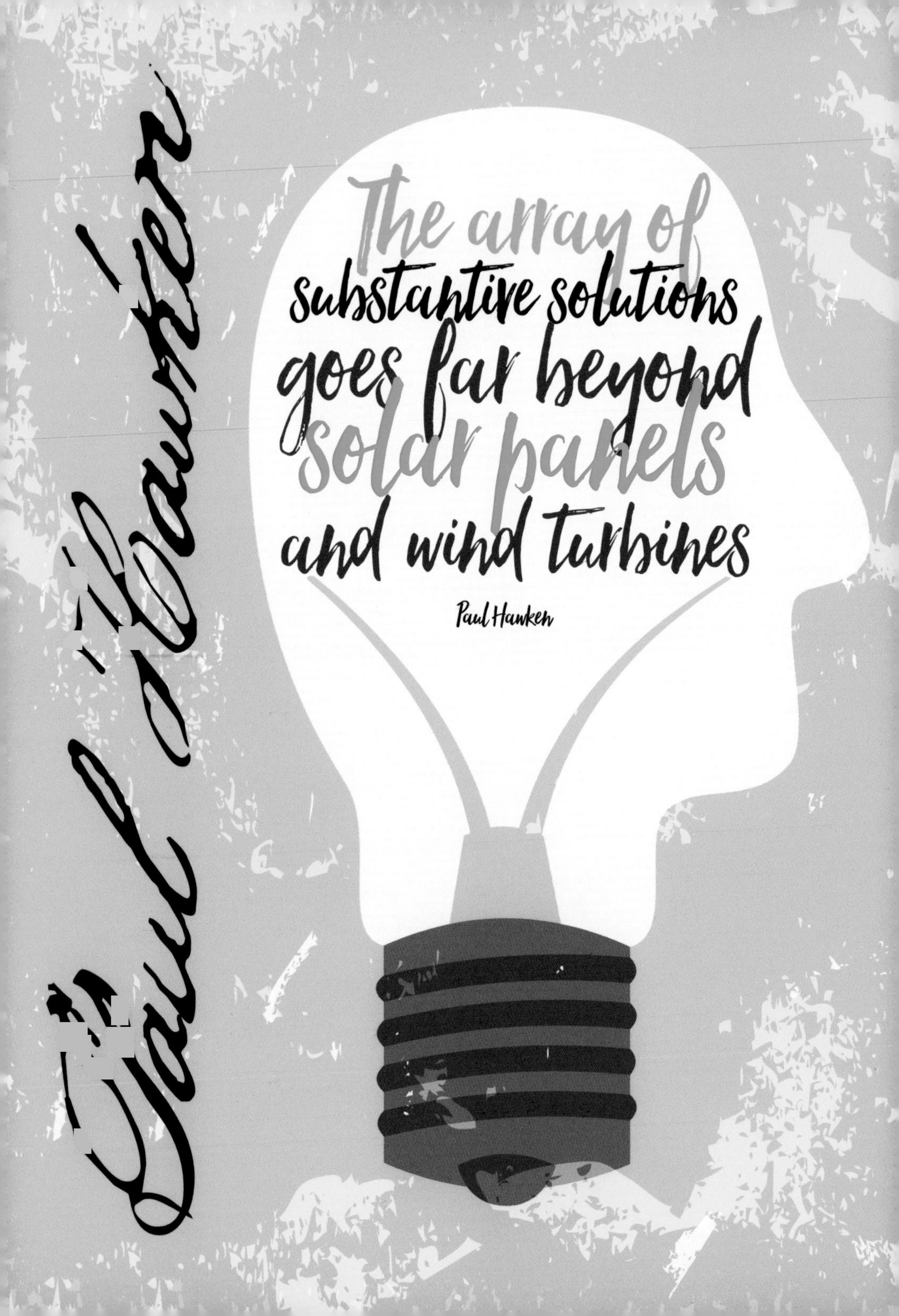

The array of substantive solutions goes far beyond solar panels and wind turbines

Paul Hawken

Paul Hawken

What animal or environmental issue gets you out of bed, and why? Climate change is the transformation that transforms everything. Will climate change hasten our demise or create a renaissance in thinking, action, and innovation? If greenhouse gas emissions continue to increase at the current rate, concentrations of gases in the atmosphere will double in the next 50 years. The current business-as-usual path will result in political, economic and food insecurity, especially for the most marginalized and historically oppressed people in the world.

What are you doing about it? With a coalition of over 200 scientists, NGOs, government agencies, analysts, companies, and partners, I created Project Drawdown with my partner Amanda Ravenhill. Drawdown, in climate terms, is the first time on a year-to-year basis where greenhouse gases decline. We want to mobilize systemic action and create a conversation about climate change that moves away from fear and apathy to collaboration and regeneration, from problem definition to problem solving. Project Drawdown is analyzing the 100 most substantive solutions to climate change and describing the atmospheric and financial impacts of these state-of-the-shelf solutions if deployed at scale over the next thirty years.

What can everyone do about it? We must begin by understanding that addressing climate change will have cascading benefits to health, prosperity, and human well-being. The array of substantive solutions goes far beyond solar panels and wind turbines. And it's all related: agro-forestry and food forests are one of the most effective ways we can feed people and bring carbon back into our soils; educating young girls in the developing world reduces birthrates and poverty, which cascades into economic stability and environmental sustainability. By understanding drawdown, we can see that climate change is not happening to us, it is happening *for* us so that we can reimagine our world and our relationship to each other and all life.

PAUL HAWKEN *has written seven books published in over 50 countries in 28 languages including four* New York Times *bestsellers,* The Next Economy, Growing a Business, The Ecology of Commerce, *and* Blessed Unrest. *He has appeared on the network TV news shows, and been profiled in the* Wall Street Journal, Newsweek, *the* Washington Post, Business Week, *and* Esquire. *He founded the first natural food company in the U.S. that relied solely on sustainable agriculture and has served on the board of many environmental organizations including Point Foundation, Center for Plant Conservation, Trust for Public Land, Conservation International, and the National Audubon Society.*

"Men argue, nature acts"
Voltaire

What animal or environmental issue gets you out of bed, and why? Genuine and mounting concern about the magnitude and the urgency of responding adequately to climate change. Voltaire commented, "Men argue, nature acts." While governments argue about adequate emission reduction targets and prevaricate about the policies they need to adopt to achieve them, nature is acting. We can and should change behavior, drive the debate, and force appropriate response at all levels of our society.

What are you doing about it? I chair The Asset Owners Disclosure Project (AODP) that surveys, rates, and ranks (names and shames) the top 1000 asset owners globally on their recognition and management of climate risks in their portfolios. At this time, those funds control some US$75 trillion. The top asset owners invest more than 55% of their funds in carbon-exposed industries, but less than 2% in low-carbon industries. Because investment will ultimately drive responses to climate change, we believe that those investments should spur something of a "technological revolution," as investment, and finance generally, shifts from carbon-exposed to low-carbon intensive industries—away from fossil fuels to renewables, energy efficiencies, and other low-carbon intensive industries. The global financial system risks a financial crisis induced by climate events, government policy responses, technological advances, or some combination of these. At some point, to paraphrase Voltaire, *finance* will act!

What can everyone do about it? Change your own behavior. Demand disclosure, analysis, and adjustment in the climate-related financial risks being run by investment funds. Remember that the directors and trustees of these funds have a clear, long-term, fiduciary responsibility to manage these funds so as to maximize their benefits over their lifetime. Ignoring or underestimating climate risks clearly compromises their responsibilities. Individuals should not underestimate the influence that they can have. Become an activist and drive the public debate to change the behavior of governments, business, banks, pension funds, et cetera.

JOHN HEWSON, Ph.D., is an economic and financial expert with experience in academia, business, government, media, and the financial system. Dr. Hewson has had several careers in academia, business, government (including as a national political leader), and as a columnist and commentator. He has started businesses in garbage recycling, energy-efficient lightbulbs, bio-diesel plants, green data centers, energy storage, refining, and generating electricity and energy from sugar cane. He is a policymaker, panelist, writer, commentator, and consultant to international agencies, has recently served as Special Advisor to the Secretary General of the UN Economic and Social Commission for Asia and the Pacific, and is a member of the Trilateral Commission.

Live
simpler,
happier
lives.

Graham Hill

What animal or environmental issue gets you out of bed, and why? Global warming is the environmental issue that gets me out of bed. It can override every other issue, whether economic, political, social, or existential. If our planet can no longer support human life due to climate instability, all other concerns will be moot. It's our responsibility to do what we can to undo the harms we have done to the planet and its other residents. This planet and its systems are so magnificent and we've consistently screwed them over. It's time we do something about that.

What are you doing about it? I've started a company, LifeEdited, to encourage architectural, design and behavioral innovation around doing more with less. We believe that by combining great design and the best technology has to offer, we can live with a lot less space and stuff, create a much smaller environmental footprint, and live simpler, happier lives. Our focus is on homes because no other single category has the power to reduce our environmental footprint to the same degree. The resources needed to build, maintain and access homes is epic. Our homes produce at least 40 percent of manmade carbon emissions and many believe that figure is as much as 70 percent. Through LifeEdited, we are building amazing, transformative homes and other spaces that do everything a larger home can, but use a fraction of the space and energy. We also have a keen interest in product design. We want our great, compact homes to be filled with less, but much better stuff. We want to create a physical world—whether it's the houses we live in or the pens we carry—that's functional, beautiful, cherished and, whenever possible, shared to its maximum extent.

What can everyone do about it? More than anything, LifeEdited is about prioritizing. At the end of the day, or at the end of our lives, the things that will most matter are our relationships and experiences, not our formal dining room or Bluetooth speakers. We can all take stock of our lives and ask, "What's truly important to me?" Then, bit by bit, we can permanently eliminate the stuff that's unimportant.

Founder and CEO of LifeEdited, GRAHAM HILL is a visionary with startup experience that has changed the world. He helped found SiteWerks and Treehugger.com. His work has been featured in many of America's leading media outlets, from the New York Times *to TED Talks. Hill has been featured on the cover of Inc. and was voted one of* Fast Company's *100 Most Creative People in Business. His projects have won both the AIA Honor and Architizer A+ Awards.*

What animal or environmental issue gets you out of bed, and why? The literal answer: Dogs. Dogs get me out of bed. Three of them, to be exact, each vying for first contact (their tongue, my face). While dogs are my morning routine, my love for animals goes from captivity to the wild and from land to sea. My love for the lot of them makes me feel protective. I wish for animals to be treated well, to have what they need to play out their lives as naturally as possible. I'd like for people to appreciate all that animals contribute to our world or, even better, to see value in their existence regardless of what they provide to us.

What are you doing about it? I'm a writer dedicated to telling animals' stories. I celebrate not just the easy-to-love creatures but the strange and peculiar, I write of the evolutionary forces that make life's messy diversity possible and I report on how animals and habitats are faring in a space bloated with humans and why it matters. I have tried to offer a peek at animal empathy. There is much to learn about what our non-human kin are capable of, but evidence indicates that they are more mentally acute than we once believed. I aim to entertain and instill hope while pushing readers to ask questions: *What are these other creatures really thinking? What emotions do we share? Why should we care?*

What can everyone do about it? Treating animals gently and with respect is an excellent place to start. Of course, it takes more than a nice gesture to keep the local shelter running or to battle habitat loss and poaching thousands of miles away. But everyone must find his or her own way to contribute, whether by giving a stray a home or something more far reaching. Some people volunteer and advocate, others write big checks, still others push for change through writing, art, and music. Diverse efforts are good for the big picture. They're good for other animals. They're good for us.

JENNIFER HOLLAND is a science writer and the author of three bestselling books about animals: Unlikely Friendships: 47 Remarkable Stories from the Animal Kingdom; Unlikely Loves: 43 Heartwarming True Stories from the Animal Kingdom; *and* Unlikely Heroes: 37 Inspiring Stories of Courage and Heart. *She is a former senior staff writer and current contributor to* National Geographic *magazine. Her articles and personal essays appear in numerous print and online publications.*

What animal or environmental issue gets you out of bed, and why? Our poor, sick Mother Earth and the suffering of the vulnerable, particularly non-human animals, as they are most vulnerable. I think about the billions of factory-farmed animals who wake up every day in misery, wild animals who succumb to habitat loss or captivity, abused animals in domestic homes, entertainment, sports, and research, and the animals who are exported live to cruel international abattoirs. We need to help animals. It's urgent because in our capacity to suffer, we're equal—what happens to them, matters to them.

What are you doing about it? I'm raising my three daughters to be compassionate, caring Earth stewards. They spent most of their childhood living on sheep and cattle stations where they developed a strong connection to nature and animals. They were taught how to handle sheep, cattle and horses in a quiet, low-stress, respectful way and developed a lifelong love of nature's beauty and power. I try to live each day with a compassionate radar and make decisions about what I buy and what I do with the intention of doing more good and less harm. I write adventure stories for 5- to 12-year-old children with humane education messages such as respect for nature, compassion to all animals, and the consequences of our choices to other life on Earth. If we are to raise good people who care about our world, humane education needs to start in early childhood.

What can everyone do about it? Wake up and take action. We need to consume less, and consume only ethical products. We need more activism and more voices for animals in schools, law, and media to create social change. Let your life AND your children be your message. As parents, we need to raise more compassionate and connected children. We need children who will grow up considering all life on earth—animals, people and ecosystems—rather than money and materialism. Wanting a better planet for our children's future is not enough. We need better children to take care of our planet.

NATALIE HOUGHTON spent decades co-managing isolated sheep and cattle stations in outback Australia where she raised her three daughters, Sophie, Eliza and Zara, with a love of the bush. Former CEO of the Jane Goodall Institute Australia, Natalie is now writing children's adventure books with humane education themes and is a director of a marketing and business consultancy company which supports organisations who are committed to helping our planet.

What animal or environmental issue gets you out of bed, and why?
Environmental stewardship jolts me into action every day. We have one world with finite resources but the human race seems to have lost sight of this. By taking more from our ecosystems and natural processes than can be replenished, we are jeopardizing our very future. We need to learn again how to live within our means, and to find ways to rejuvenate, restore and regenerate the natural world wherever we can.

What are you doing about it? Since first exploring Cambodia's Koh Rong Archipelago nearly a decade ago, my husband Rory and I have devoted our energies to protecting its coral reefs and helping local villagers. We founded the Song Saa Foundation (an independent NGO devoted to the environmental and social welfare of the region) and Song Saa Private Island, a luxury resort with a focus on restoring and protecting the environment. When we first came across the two islands, which are now known collectively as Song Saa, we had no plans to establish an NGO or a resort, and we simply began by picking up rubbish. In those early days, over-fishing had caused fish-stocks to collapse and forced villagers into the jungles to log the rainforest and poach wildlife for food. By working with local village chiefs, we established Cambodia's first protected marine area on the reef surrounding the 'Song Saa' islands. Today, it is the largest marine park in the Gulf of Thailand. We've also established social welfare initiatives with local communities, including a solid waste management system and a number of alternative livelihood projects. Our work is "place based" and "needs focused," and we continue to be guided by the locals in all that we do.

What can everyone do about it? We must work harder to live within our means and think every day about whether or not we are achieving that. Listen to other people's stories and allow yourself to be moved by people, places, and what others are doing to protect them. By doing this, paths can open up for us and lead us to unexpected places.

MELITA HUNTER is a multi-award winning artist, designer, and businesswoman, and a leader in ethical development in Southeast Asia's tourism markets. She is the co-founder and director of the Song Saa Foundation and the creative mind behind the architecture, master planning, and interior design of Song Saa Private Island in Cambodia's Koh Rong Archipelago. Melita believes development can bring multiple benefits to an area if it is conducted in a way that is rejuvenating, ethical, and nurturing.

What animal or environmental issue gets you out of bed, and why? I am passionately driven to improve the world my children will inherit. I worry about elephants, primates, and youth education. Elephant populations are in rapid decline due to the high demand for ivory in Asia. (Most individuals have no idea that ivory comes from dead elephants—they don't understand and the effects of their ignorance are so devastating—100,000 elephants were killed in the last three years and only around 400,000 remain.) And the great apes are victims of habitat loss and the illegal wildlife trade. They are captured, traded, and sold as pets but primates are incredibly smart and often cause more trouble than the buyers anticipated. They are often left to rot and die in cages. For every animal sold, there are many more who don't make it to the market and die in captivity. But unless people are aware of what's happening in the world around us it's difficult to inspire change.

What are you doing about it? In 2006, I founded Green Kampong, an online resource about sustainable living. Together with Dr. Tammie Matson, I created the documentary *Let Elephants Be Elephants* that aims to reduce the demand for ivory in Asia. We also created a series of webisodes and I lecture across the region. I joined Jane Goodall and Richard Leakey as an ambassador for the UN Great Apes Survival Partnership (UN-GRASP). I am currently researching a similar project for orangutans. And I am currently a member of the Green School board of directors.

What can everyone do about it? The most important thing that any of us can do is educate ourselves to the realities of our world. Understand where things come from, how they are made, and where they go to when we are done with them. Understand the impacts of consumption. Find a cause that resonates with you and get on board to support it in any way that you can. A small drop in the ocean can make large and far reaching ripples. Never think you are not big enough to create change.

*Eco-activist and media personality **NADYA HUTAGALUNG** is one of Asia's leading voices in the Green Movement.*

Rukshan Jayewardene

What animal or environmental issue gets you out of bed, and why? If there is one animal that will get me out of bed more than any other animal on earth, it is the leopard. The leopard is beautiful, intelligent, agile, strong, courageous, wily, elusive, stealthy, and resourceful. It is a great mammalian survivor – the most resilient and adaptable of all the big cats.

What are you doing about it? I had the good fortune of being part of a team that produced the first book exclusively dedicated to the Sri Lankan leopard, in order to raise the profile and create awareness of this unique sub-species that is native only to this one island. We also established The Leopard Trust to further the conservation of this under-appreciated and poorly understood animal. Towards this end, all contributions to this book were donated and the proceeds were used where most needed in the field. Lately I have been involved in a camera-trap study which aims to understand leopard distribution and relationships in a population that lives in a circumscribed area in the country's most popular national park, Yala.

What can everyone do about it? Everyone can learn more about the leopard; today there is more knowledge, information, and opportunity than when our book first came out in 2003. The leopard is much more than a charismatic animal that graces national parks and reserves and is much sought after by both locals and tourists. It is an all-important predator that helps to maintain the equilibrium of the eco-systems that it inhabits. This is particularly true for Sri Lanka where it is the top carnivore. The first steps toward the 'need' to conserve are awareness and appreciation. Hopefully organizations and individuals will channel the resulting goodwill to further the long-term conservation of the species. It is also hoped that the younger generation will produce inspired individuals and mechanisms that will succeed in the conservation of leopards, despite the many priorities of a fast developing, densely populated nation.

RUKSHAN JAYEWARDENE resides in Sri Lanka, and chairs the Wilderness & Protected Areas Foundation. He is a vice-president of the Wildlife & Nature Protection Society, joint-president of the Wildlife Conservation Forum, a trustee of The Leopard Trust, and a director of Environmental Foundation Ltd (EFL). EFL is the primary organization taking legal action against violators of 'environmental laws, including the government of Sri Lanka. He is part of the photo collective Threeblindmen. Rukshan is interested in all biodiversity and conservation-related issues, specifically the long-term conservation of the Sri Lankan leopard.

What animal or environmental issue gets you out of bed, and why? I am realizing lately that the hardest thing to bear is not all the destruction and bad news, it is the immense and overwhelming beauty of our world. The more we learn about the multi-scalar and multi-dimensional cosmic dance that is happening around us all the time, the more astonishing and mysterious it becomes. In this emotional/ spiritual space, we begin to comprehend the enormity of the gift we have each been given, and this connects us with our gratitude, love, and wisdom. What if humanity could find the courage to stand in awe together and remember what we have forgotten about the incomprehensibly amazing miracle that we are all part of?

What are you doing about it? Mostly I just follow around behind my camera as it pulls me ever deeper into the woods. And I love speaking about my work; it is always a privilege to talk at schools and gatherings. There are so many inspiring and engaged people in the world, especially today's youth; being with them is like plugging into a spiritual battery charger.

What can everyone do about it? One of my Buddhist friends taught me this: when you wake up in the morning, the first moment that you become conscious, maybe even before you open your eyes, just take a few seconds to feel the thrill of realizing that you are alive. Wow.

CHRIS JORDAN is a photographic artist based in Seattle, Washington, USA. His work explores contemporary mass culture from a variety of photographic and conceptual perspectives, connecting the viewer viscerally to the enormity and power of humanity's collective unconscious. He asks us to look both inward and outward at the traumatized landscapes of our collective choices. Chris's work reaches an increasingly broad international audience through his exhibitions, books, website, interviews on radio and television, and speaking engagements and school visits all over the world.

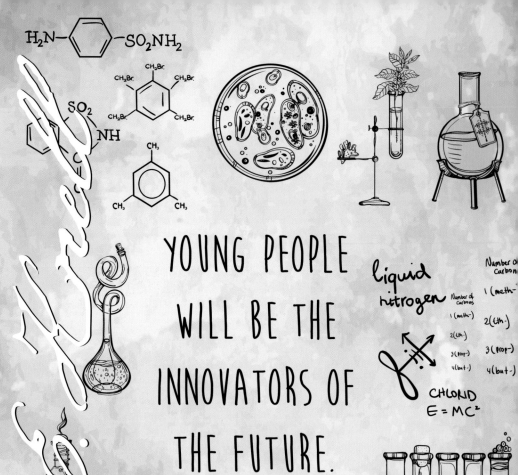

YOUNG PEOPLE
WILL BE THE
INNOVATORS OF
THE FUTURE.

GARY E. KNELL

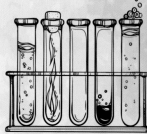

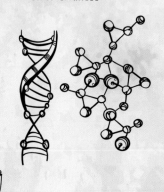

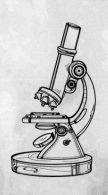

What animal or environmental issue gets you out of bed, and why? I think often about the air we breathe. We can't take that—or so many other aspects of our environment—for granted. I grew up breathing dirty air in Los Angeles, where a strong community effort eventually improved air quality for kids and families. If we work together, we can make positive changes on a larger scale—global changes—to improve our environment and our lives.

What are you doing about it? At the National Geographic Society, we believe in the power of science and exploration to change the world. We have identified three core issue areas we will cover in our various media platforms and support through grants to explorers and scientists working around the world. The first is the ocean. The vast majority of the ocean is unprotected and unexplored, and most people are unaware of how essential it is to all life on earth. The second initiative is wildlife. Building off of successful programs like our Big Cats Initiative, we want to expose the tremendous threats that iconic species are facing. And the third, saving our past. We want to protect the material remains of the past, which are under threat from a combination of site destruction, trafficking of antiquities and fossils, environmental degradation, and more.

What can everyone do about it? We could not be National Geographic without our members, partners, readers, and students and teachers who participate in our programs. Working together, I am confident our best days are ahead of us if we recommit ourselves to making an impact on the world. I think it's particularly important to seek out and understand the world around you so you can make good decisions and be a responsible citizen of this planet. This means instilling in our young people the attributes they need to be good citizens of the world—intellectual curiosity, critical thinking, problem solving, creativity, and responsibility. They will be the innovators of the future.

GARY E. KNELL brings decades of experience in media and education to his role as president and CEO of National Geographic, where he has advanced the organization's work around science, exploration, and storytelling. The brand reaches 700 million worldwide, with 150 million followers across social media platforms. He has worked to elevate geography education, with a new learning framework to encourage global awareness in K–12 students. Knell was CEO of NPR from 2011 to 2013. Prior, he spent 22 years at Sesame Workshop, where he was appointed CEO in 2000. He has a J.D. from Loyola University and a B.A. from UCLA.

What animal or environmental issue gets you out of bed, and why? The single issue that gets me out of bed (or prevents me from falling asleep) is climate change. The science makes it increasingly clear that anthropogenic climate change is happening, and that the risks associated with only a 2-degree temperature rise are bigger than we realized. The impact of such warming on biodiversity and habitats, on poverty and hunger, and on extreme weather and health will make this planet far less welcoming for future generations than it has been for us. With four children, and one day hopefully some grandkids, I feel that addressing climate change is the moral challenge of our generation.

What are you doing about it? As CEO of Rocky Mountain Institute (RMI) and Carbon War Room (CWR), I am privileged to be part of one of the most passionate teams of energy professionals working on the energy revolution to create a clean, prosperous, and secure energy future. RMI, founded in 1982 by my colleague Amory Lovins, has been on the forefront of driving energy efficiency and supporting the deployment of renewable energy for almost 35 years. In 2014, we merged with CWR, founded by Sir Richard Branson and a group of likeminded entrepreneurs to advance a low-carbon economy. At RMI-CWR we work with utilities and clean tech companies to accelerate the role of solar and wind in the electricity system. We work extensively to make buildings more efficient and collaborate with other organizations to pilot new models of personal mobility across cities in the U.S., and together with Chinese authorities, we have plotted a path towards low-carbon prosperity for China.

What can everyone do about it? Switching to a low carbon lifestyle is now within reach for most of us. Energy efficiency has always been an economic proposition, but now LED lamps, hybrid cars, and superior insulation make it even more so. Putting solar panels on your roof now makes sense in much of the developed world, and in many places you can do it with no money down. Switching to a diet less based on red meat is a matter of habit and saves a lot of carbon. And above all, we must all consider the implication of climate change when we cast our vote. We have no excuse anymore and no time to waste: we all have to roll up our sleeves to make a low-carbon future a reality.

JULES KORTENHORST, *CEO of Rocky Mountain Institute and Carbon War Room, works to transforms global energy use to create a clean, prosperous, and secure low-carbon future.*

Ron Lameman

What animal or environmental issue gets you out of bed, and why? Canada's provincial and national governments are licensing multi and transnational corporations to extract bitumen from traditional Cree territory. These permits violate the international Nation to Nation Treaty my ancestors entered into with the Crown in 1876. The Treaty guarantees our Nation the right continue our way of life—to hunt, fish, trap, and gather within our traditional territories—for "as long as the sun shines, the grass grows and the rivers flow." Our Elders teach us that the plants, animals, the rocks, air and water are our older siblings. Our older siblings were here first and promised the Creator they would take care of us. We must hold them in high regard and treat all of Creation with respect. These treaty violations devastate our environment, our family.

What are you doing about it? For more than 35 years, I have worked on United Nations committees and councils, acting on behalf of the rights of our Peoples and our once-pristine environment. I raised concerns about the devastation of the tar sands in northern Alberta, and with my brother, the former Chief of the Beaver Lake Cree Nation Al Lameman, I challenged the legality of the more than 17,000 permits granted by our governments to multi- and transnational corporations who are raping and pillaging our Mother Earth. And I serve on the board of the RAVEN (Respecting Aboriginal Values and Environmental Needs) Trust, which offers financial support to Indigenous Nations who have legally challenged governments and corporations involved in the degradation and destruction of the environment.

What can everyone do about it? Look into your everyday life and see where you, as an individual, can make adjustments to prevent further degradation of the environment. Assess who and what you support with your shopping habits, your vote, and what you are teaching your children. We must appreciate what our ancestors have done for us, go forward in a respectful manner, and build a legacy for our future generations. Our children, grandchildren, and great grandchildren are our most precious resource—as are the water and air, and Mother Earth who sustains us all.

RON LAMEMAN is a citizen of the Beaver Lake Cree Nation, Treaty No. 6 Territory, Alberta, Canada. He is a lifetime proponent of the Treaty, upholding and enforcing the Rights of the Indigenous Nations in Alberta and Saskatchewan, Canada, and representing the interests and concerns of Indigenous Peoples around the world. In addition to serving as the Bilateral Treaty Coordinator, Ron works with the Elders and leadership of the Confederacy of Treaty Six First Nations.

Harvey Locke

What animal or environmental issue gets you out of bed, and why? I am in love with wild nature. Since childhood, Banff National Park in the Canadian Rockies has been a place of spiritual importance to me. I am lucky to now live here, surrounded by wild things and wild beauty every day. I am also enchanted by tigers in India, elephants in Africa, and bowerbirds in Australia. The Earth is a beautiful place and my waking dream is to restore a functional and loving relationship between humanity and the rest of nature. Scientific assessments in many varied ecosystems on many continents indicate that in order to maintain all of wild nature in a flourishing condition we ought to protect at least half of the world in an interconnected way.

What are you doing about it? In the Yellowstone to Yukon Region of North America, I work to create national parks and wilderness areas, conserve private and public lands that connect them, and create crossing structures for wildlife over busy highways so both wildlife and people can thrive. At the global level, through the Nature Needs Half movement, I support the work of colleagues on other continents who have similar goals. I engage people with wild nature through photography and by writing articles and books, traveling widely on speaking tours, and appearing in films that are produced in a variety of countries.

What can everyone do about it? We all need to have the moral courage to free ourselves from the domineering economic mindset that insists current patterns of environmental abuse are inevitable. The economy serves society, not the other way around. We can get our society back on course by remembering that we are one species among many and that, like all of life, we are wholly dependent on the atmosphere for the air we breathe, the biosphere for the food we eat, and the hydrosphere for the water we drink. We need to give ourselves permission to speak our values out loud and to describe the world we want to live in. If we combine positive aspiration with hard work then hope will be restored and change for the better will follow.

HARVEY LOCKE is a conservationist, writer, and photographer. He is a global leader in the field of parks, wilderness, and large landscape conservation. A founder of the Yellowstone to Yukon Conservation Initiative and the Nature Needs Half movement, Locke was named one of Canada's leaders for the 21st century by Time *Magazine Canada and was awarded IUCN's Fred M. Packard Award for his service to the world's protected areas.*

The life

of the

"pragmatic

idealist"

requires

one

vital

ingredient.

hope.

Simon Longstaff

Simon Longstaff

What animal or environmental issue gets you out of bed, and why? Ethics. There was once a time when we were confident enough in our ethical judgement to let arguments about good, bad, right or wrong rest on ethics alone, when notions of "stewardship" and a simple regard for the intrinsic value of other people and forms of life was sufficient, when an appeal to "enlightened self-interest" was not thought to be the clinching argument in any discussion. But our ethical standards have become couched in the language of economics and we have ultimately reduced ethical considerations to a cost/benefit analysis. Our reckless indifference to humanity's impact on the planet and the unconscionable cruelty that we introduce into the lives of other sentient creatures moves me, but I worry most about our loss of confidence in the language of ethics that would enable a deeper conversation about such matters.

What are you doing about it? I work with others to bring new life to popular engagement with ethical issues. The concepts of "ethics" need to be rescued from the realm of the "worthy" and brought back to what is simply *worthwhile*. We are trying to grow people's capacity to be and do good, to help people re-learn the universal grammar of choice that shapes everything that humans do in and to the world. We are still learning how to make the connections. There is little to be gained by lecturing or preaching to people, but if we can but show people what is done "in our name," then we will often engage in a conversation which leads people to rethink life's most important questions.

What can everyone do about it? The first (and easiest) step is to ask questions about the ethical dimensions of what we do in the world. The second step is not to accept a glib economic response. Ethics is "the art of doing." The life of the "pragmatic idealist" requires one vital ingredient: hope. While religion may provide hope "for the world to come," ethics ultimately provides hope "in the world today." Every small action taken in support of what is "good" and "right" affirms that such choices are possible—and sometimes knowing this is enough.

SIMON LONGSTAFF, AO, PhD, has served governments and corporations. Prior to becoming the inaugural executive director of The St. James Ethics Centre in 1991, Simon consulted for Cambridge Commonwealth and Overseas Trusts. Simon served as the president of the Australian Association for Professional & Applied Ethics and is a fellow of the World Economic Forum. He is a consultant, lecturer, and leader addressing ethical issues around the world.

Richard Low

What animal or environmental issue gets you out of bed, and why? The human costs of alienation from nature – diminished use of the senses, attention difficulties, higher rates of physical and emotional illnesses, a rising rate of myopia, obesity, Vitamin D deficiency and other maladies. It's a condition I call "nature-deficit disorder."

What are you doing about it? I have written eight books about the connections between family, nature, and community including *Last Child in the Woods: Saving Our Children from Nature-Deficit Disorder and The Nature Principle: Human Restoration and the End of Nature-Deficit Disorder*. I also co-founded the Children & Nature Network and I speak to audiences nationally and internationally.

What can everyone do about it? As parents, grandparents, aunts or uncles, educators, we all can spend more time with children in nature. Health care professionals, housing developers and policy makers can recognize that as we restore nature, we restore ourselves. We can create new natural habitats in and around our homes, schools, neighborhoods, workplaces, cities and suburbs so that even in inner cities our children grow up in nature—not *with* it, but *in* it.

RICHARD LOUV *is the author of* The Nature Principle *and* Last Child in the Woods: Saving Our Children from Nature-Deficit Disorder. *He is also the co-founder and chairman emeritus of the Children & Nature Network.*

Do something,
no matter
how small.
There is
significance
and comfort
in the
positivity
of the
action.

Shirley Manson

What animal or environmental issue gets you out of bed, and why? I am obsessed by animals and I am obsessed with the environment, with climate change, sustainability, preservation, and protecting endangered species the world over. I cannot fully explain my love of animals without sounding like a complete lunatic but suffice it to say I feel deeply connected to them in every way. As for the environment… well, you can't care for animals without caring about the safeguarding of nature.

What are you doing about it? I adopted a dog off the streets of South Central LA. That was something tangible I could do. I donate regularly to a variety of animal rescue services and I have been a keen supporter of the World Wildlife Fund since I was a little girl, which covers all bases if you ask me. Climate change, sustainability, and preservation along with protecting endangered species the world over. My dream job is to work for them.

What can everyone do about it? Do something, no matter how small. There is significance and comfort in the positivity of the action. It encourages others to do the same and together we can make huge changes benefiting so many and so much. The problem for some is that they get overwhelmed by the enormity of animal or environmental issues. They get paralyzed. So I guess what I am trying to say here is, little efforts accomplished *en masse* make huge differences. Offer simple kindness and respect to an animal. Donate to your favorite cause (mine is the World Wildlife Fund). Keep a compost bin or pile in your garden. Stop using plastic bags and bottles. Don't buy plastic toys. Turn lights off when not in the room. Be conscious of waste. Walk or cycle. Recycle. Recycle. Recycle. It's simple, really. Isn't it?

SHIRLEY MANSON *is allegedly a musician and lead singer of the alt-rock band garbage. At least her passport describes her occupation that way. She has also been known to play a terminator robot on TV. She tries to be a good person, good friend, wife, sister, daughter, bandmate, neighbor, and citizen of the world, but despite her best efforts, fails and falls short of the mark most of the time. Don't hold it against her. She really does try her best.*

What animal or environmental issue gets you out of bed, and why? My passion and purpose in life is protecting water, our most precious resource. Fresh water on earth is finite, be it from underground aquifers, rivers, creeks, streams or snowmelt from the mountains. Many of us in the developed world only see water coming out of a tap. We have a duty to protect and preserve the environment and fresh water from complacent governments, rapacious mining companies, and ignorant individuals.

What are you doing about it? Eight years ago, I joined the Save Water Alliance to lobby against the New South Wales government's plans to pump water from a highly vulnerable aquifer in the Southern Highlands to provide just three days of water to Sydney. We won. Recently, I've been fighting a major underground coal mine in our district, which would have a catastrophic impact on the aquifer that provides our water. It's been all-consuming and we're now helping many other communities in the fight against fossil fuel extraction.

What can everyone do about it? Engage the people in the cities, help them understand that this affects them too and that rural communities can't fight this alone. Demand that governments make long-term strategic decisions to protect our water and the environment. If the mismanagement continues in the name of "development," future generations will pay a terrible cost as others around the world are now finding out.

KIM MARTIN is a mother of four adult children, a farmer, passionate cook, gardener, and now an environmental activist. She loves exercise, traveling and reading but most of all her garden and her family.

What animal or environmental issue gets you out of bed, and why? This waterhole is near where the last dead specimen of the thought-to-be-extinct Night Parrot was collected and near where live specimens were sighted in 2014. The Night Parrot's demise was the result of two centuries of slow violence from feral cats and grazing pressure. Filmmaker Rob Nutall interviewed me at this waterhole. I talked about the sublime nature of extinction and whether the Night Parrot, if indeed rediscovered, would succumb to the sixth extinction. It's possible. New anthropocentric drivers help place Australia at the top of the global list for mammalian extinction. Since visiting this waterhole, a small group of Night Parrots was rediscovered and is being monitored. One of them has already been killed by a feral cat.

What are you doing about it? Using the slow technology of paint, I give people cause for soul searching about our human folly. Glenn Albrecht coined a neologism for the sort of landscape grieving we develop as these landscapes disappear as a result of too much environmental change, *solastalgia*. The sublime helps me picture the inconceivable and mediate the grief I feel about irreversible global change. The powdery blacks, blazing light and chunky texture in my painting are seductive, even though the painting refers to death and extinction. The connection between place and spiritual being is especially strong within the ancient and continuous culture of Aboriginal Australians, who in fact call the 'Night Parrot' the 'Morning Parrot.'

What can everyone do about it? We must stem our insatiable greed, develop humility towards other organisms, and start living lightly on this land. We need to understand the price of exploitation and what it means to lose our landscapes. We need to create non-conventional alliances between all other stakeholders. Time is running out!

MANDY MARTIN, a renowned environmental artist, has held numerous exhibitions in Australia and internationally. Her works are in many public and private collections including the National Gallery of Australia, the state collections, and many regional galleries. In the USA, she is represented in the Guggenheim Museum New York, the Los Angeles Museum of Contemporary Art, and the Center for Art + Environment collections of the Nevada Museum of Art. She lives in Central Western New South Wales and is an Adjunct Professor, Fenner School of Environment and Society, Australian National University. Since 1995, she has initiated and participated in ten art and environment projects, including the current project Arnhembrand: Living on Healthy Country.

Dinosaurs

Plants

Bugs

Science

Animals

Discover

Fossils

Enjoy the nature within your neighborhood
(sometimes you'll find it right down the block.)
Juan Martinez

Juan Martinez

What animal or environmental issue gets you out of bed, and why? The next generation of nature-smart leaders and the hope that they will carry the legacy we're building forward. We have a tremendous legacy of conservation, outdoor recreation, and science, but I think that sometimes the narrative of *people* gets lost. Often you'll see a photo of a polar bear and that photo represents the narrative for climate change. I want to make sure that the next generation understands that the links connecting that polar bear and climate change to oil prices—and why creating renewable energy, conserving wild and open spaces, and urban planning and urban agriculture—are important to all of us, now and in the future.

What are you doing about it? I've created The Natural Leaders Network. Every year we gather young people from all over the world for a week of intensive leadership training aimed at bringing their own communities together and engaging with open spaces in their neighborhoods and cities. We work to develop community action plans that include partnership, service, jobs and outdoor recreation. In every community, these four themes look different, but working collectively, we can help each other solve our problems.

What can everyone do about it? Step forward and lead. Begin with your neighbors, talk to your family, your cousins and your friends. Invite people to join you outside, slow down and enjoy the nature within your neighborhood (sometimes you'll find it right down the block; sometimes it's just a bus ride away.) Invite the family next door on an outing, put beehives on your roof, or install solar panels. If we're able to engage tomorrow's leaders and outdoor enthusiasts with technology and entertainment, and give them the power to create the change that they want to create, then I think we'll indeed pass on our legacy as guides and stewards.

*A National Geographic Explorer, TED Speaker, and a proud product of South Central Los Angeles, **JUAN D. MARTINEZ** is Children and Nature Network's director of leadership development and the Natural Leaders Network. His passion to empower young individuals led him to direct Sierra Club's first environmental justice youth leadership academy in Los Angeles. Juan was named a National Geographic Emerging Explorer in 2011. In 2014, he was recognized by the National Science Teachers Association's Multicultural and Equity Committee for his work as a Global Explorer. He works with strategic partners and grassroots leaders to empower the next generation of conservation and outdoor recreation leaders and create positive change.*

What animal or environmental issue gets you out of bed, and why? There's an invisible war being waged against animals. We humans enslave millions of animals every single day through our consumer habits. We eat them, wear them, use products and medicines that are tested on them, and we use them for our entertainment as well. Although animals make up a part of our daily lives, they remain invisible to us. The amount of suffering they endure at our hands has reached unfathomable proportions. It's an emergency and I treat it as such.

What are you doing about it? I'm using my skills as a photojournalist to make the world a kinder place for animals. The camera is a powerful tool for change, and I use it to document the way animals live and die behind the walls of factory farms, fur farms, laboratories, and slaughterhouses, and the way we use them for entertainment, such as at aquariums, roadside zoos, rodeos, and circuses. Photos illustrate what goes on behind closed doors, and only if we become better informed about animal abuse can we make more ethical decisions about what—and whom—we consume. I try to show that animals aren't just an anonymous mass of faceless creatures. "*A million animals*" is, after all, comprised of *individuals* . . . one then another, then another . . . and they all need our help.

What can everyone do about it? We can be *actively* kind and compassionate. We can stop consuming animals. We can use our skills, whatever they may be, to make the world a kinder place. Consider *who* is affected by the choices you make. Consider *who* is on your plate and what kind of life they must have had. Incorporate this consideration into absolutely everything you do. Ask yourself every day, *how can I help others*? You *can* help. Every single one of your actions count.

JO-ANNE McARTHUR is a photojournalist and educator whose goal in life is to help animals through her long-term project, We Animals*. Jo-Anne travels the globe documenting our uses, abuses and sharing of spaces with our non-human kin. She contributes to organizations, academia, and campaigns advocating for animals. Jo-Anne is also the subject of the award-winning Canadian documentary* The Ghosts in Our Machine

What animal or environmental issue gets you out of bed, and why? Trees are plants of great beauty and utility. I actively promote tree preservation and propagation. They provide oxygen, shade, firewood, fruit, toilet paper, furniture, building construction materials and much more. I encourage the sustainable industrial utilization of trees.

What are you doing about it? We have created a National Register of Big Trees. This catalogue of the trees of every species in Australia is an impressive way to entice people to visit—and honor—the champion trees. Using the American Forests' National Register of Big Trees' 80-year-old formula of measurement, it is possible to make holistic comparisons between Australia's big trees. The Register records these champion trees in our gardens, parks, and rural properties.

What can everyone do about it? Talk tree talk! All communities have comprehensive legislation and guidelines for the protection and expansion of forests and parklands so there is little to do on this front. Become a financial supporter of a tree-planting organization, such as TreeProject – they have the volunteers but never enough money. We urban dwellers can make a significant contribution by becoming involved in local Bushcare bushland regeneration activities. They do amazing work with the planting of trees and plants. The majority of rural property owners are committed tree custodians and tend the trees on a daily basis – perhaps an additional ten trees planted per year is what they can do about it. Planting trees is easy; the difficult part is the ongoing protection and maintenance of young trees.

DEREK McINTOSH is a life-long tree aficionado. As a tree-climbing kid in South Africa, he quickly learned that African acacias were not good trees to climb due to the thorns and the imported and widely grown gum trees were impossible to climb due to their trunks with no branches. This was the start of his love affair with trees. Now, using the American Forests' National Register of Big Trees' 80 year old formula of measurement, he makes holistic comparisons between big trees and all that they provide.

Jo McIntyre

What animal or environmental issue gets you out of bed, and why? Invasive mining of our natural resources for short-term economic gain. Coal seam gas (CSG) and coal mining companies, supported by state and federal governments of all persuasions, are irreversibly transforming huge swathes of Australia.

What are you doing about it? I research and make art to spark others' concern about what's really happening. Mining sites are locked and guarded and exploration sites sealed off. We cannot fly over them or get close enough to see for ourselves the devastating, overall impacts on our precious rural communities, water, land, vegetation and heritage. Satellite photos only hint at the real extent of the scars, loss and devastation. I want to show what's actually happening at ground level, from the destruction of our forests, bushland, and productive farmland to the polluted rivers and aquifers, the air and noise pollution and the impacts on people. I now understand that when politicians and mining interests ride roughshod over us we have no choice but to fight back.

What can everyone do about it? Join a community-based organization in which business people, the young, the elderly, greenies, farmers, workers, medicos, other professionals, academics, artists and retirees pool their different skills, working together in strong new mining and fracking resistance groups. Information and knowledge, combined with creativity and art, make powerful weapons. Important in this armoury of skills and knowledge are photography, filmmaking, song writing, knitting, writing, art and design. Fighting is energizing. Creative activities further unite and empower us.

JO McINTYRE *For over 30 years, Jo has had a long and satisfying career at the State Library of New South Wales. In her art, she draws most inspiration from where she lives, currently in the country south of Sydney.*

NEVER
UNDERESTIMATE
A VEGAN
HIPPIE CHICK
WITH A
RACE CAR

LEILANI MÜNTER

Leilani Münter

What animal or environmental issue gets you out of bed, and why? Promoting a vegan diet. Every year, the meat industry slaughters ten billion animals for food in the U.S. and raising animals for food generates more greenhouse gas emissions than the entire direct impact of the transportation sector. With a plant-based diet we save animals and reduce our carbon footprint and it's good for our health. It's a win-win-win for the planet, animals, and our bodies.

What are you doing about it? I believe that it's extremely important for environmental and animal rights activists to get out and speak to people who don't agree with us. If we only work with people who believe in the same things that we do, then who's going to change the minds of those who don't? I'm a biology graduate and I race cars professionally. On the track, I can reach out to an audience of 75 million U.S. race fans. The race car gives me a "voice" to promote my causes. Through racing I am able to reach millions of people that would never hear me if I was just a biology graduate without a race car.

What can everyone do about it? I encourage everyone to give up meat and dairy and if that feels too difficult at first, please reduce your intake of meat and dairy. Sometimes it is easier to make the transition slowly. I have a friend who after I talked about all the issues around meat, decided to make his first two meals of the day vegan. For his last meal, he could eat whatever he wanted. He told me that he has since found that he has many fully vegan days because when dinner comes around, he doesn't want meat or he chooses a vegan meal even though it's no part of his rules. Do whatever works for you, but I have found that since I went vegan I feel healthier than ever!

LEILANI MÜNTER is a biology-graduate-turned-professional race car driver and environmental activist. Discovery's Planet Green named her the #1 eco athlete in the world, ELLE *Magazine awarded her their Genius Award, and* Sports Illustrated *named her one of the top ten female race car drivers in the world. Since 2007, Leilani has adopted an acre of rainforest for every race she runs. Leilani sits on the Board of the Oceanic Preservation Society and the advisory board of The Solutions Project. Off track, Leilani drives a 100% electric car charged by the solar panels on her house. Leilani's motto is never underestimate a vegan hippie chick with a race car.*

What animal or environmental issue gets you out of bed, and why? Food, because I eat! I first learned about genetically modified (GM) crops and food 20 years ago when my first daughter was one. I thought GM foods would reduce pesticide use so I was initially supportive. I started researching GM and the more I learned the more concerned I became. So far, the GM experiment has resulted in vast GM corn and soy monocultures, super pests, super weeds, ever-increasing pesticide use, deforestation in Latin America, and corporate control over seeds.

What are you doing about it? I co-founded MADGE, which stands for "Mothers Are Demystifying Genetic Engineering" as well as "Mothers Advocating Deliciously Good Eating." Our aim is to alert people to the disturbing and hidden changes food manufacturers make and encourage people to source food from farmers and companies who are honest about how it is grown and made.

What can everyone do about it? What we eat changes the world. Our current industrial food system produces junk food that leads to obesity, hunger, huge pesticide use, farmer debt, disease-prone monocultures, and climate change. We can reverse all this by supporting local, diverse food systems that rely on skilled farmers growing delicious food in ways that regenerate the soil and revitalize communities. Grow, swap, shop, share, cook, and eat yourself into an inspiring future.

FRAN MURRELL co-founded MADGE, a group of mothers and others trying to sort through the spin on GM food. She researches the food system and encourages people to choose food that is good for those who eat it, grow it, produce, and sell it, and for land and the environment. She has spoken on this topic nationally and internationally.

What animal or environmental issue gets you out of bed, and why? Our knowledge of how wild animal populations are impacted by environmental change is limited. Understanding how rates of cancer, congenital disorders, infectious diseases and other pathology are impacted by climate change, endocrine disrupting chemicals, and other factors is crucially important to both human and animal populations.

What are you doing about it? I co-authored *Zoobiquity: The Astonishing Connection Between Human and Animal Health*. I am trying to bring greater awareness to the diseases of wild animal populations by creating Zoobiquity conferences in which physicians and veterinarians come together to discuss the diseases shared by different species. By building bridges between medical schools and veterinary schools, I am encouraging the human health community to pay closer attention to wild populations

What can everyone do about it? An increased awareness of the role environment plays in the health and disease in wild populations can help us all recognize the crucial role a healthy environment plays in the health of our communities and families.

DR. NATTERSON-HOROWITZ is a professor of medicine in the Division of Cardiology at the David Geffen School of Medicine at UCLA. She also holds a professorship in the UCLA Department of Ecology and Evolutionary Biology and is co-director of the Evolutionary Medicine Program at UCLA. In 2012, Dr. Natterson-Horowitz co-authored the New York Times *bestselling book,* Zoobiquity: The Astonishing Connection Between Human and Animal Health. *She also serves as a cardiovascular consultant to the Los Angeles Zoo as a member of its Medical Advisory Board.*

BE BRAVE.
IT INVITES
SOMEBODY
ELSE TO BE
BRAVE TOO.

Robyn O'Brien

ROBYN O'BRIEN

What animal or environmental issue gets you out of bed, and why? The health of our children. In the U.S., our kids have earned the title 'Generation Rx' because of conditions and diseases like food allergies, autism, diabetes, obesity, and pediatric cancer. Our food supply is loaded with artificial ingredients and ingredients that didn't even exist twenty years ago. Today, in the U.S., cancer is the leading cause of death by disease in children under the age of fifteen. One in sixty-eight kids is autistic, one in ten has asthma, one in thirteen food allergies. It doesn't matter who you are, it's hitting all of us.

What are you doing about it? I am a financial analyst, I covered the food industry and learned why decisions were made to take the real ingredients out and swap in cheaper artificial ingredients (it was to drive profitability and margins). I wrote a book, *The Unhealthy Truth*. And I work with corporations, nonprofits, and consumers around the world to create a better food system. When I speak to parents, communities and corporations, I lead with data and share the financial impact disease is having on our families and economy and the food awakening that it is creating. I work with grocery store chains and global conglomerates to develop safer supply chains and understand new revenue opportunities. I listen to others who are fighting the same fight. We're beginning to move the needle, but it's a slow process. I see the growth in pediatric hospitals here in the U.S. and around the world. Globally, children are less than 30% of the population but they're 100% of our future. If we want a healthy future, we need healthy children.

What can everyone do about it? Don't make the perfect the enemy of the good. On any given day, at any given time, it's going to look different to all of us, so do your *one thing*. Be brave, it invites somebody else to be brave too. If you can, find a friend to do it with. Remember that none of us can do everything but all of us can do something. And if you have a friend that is doing something different than you are, listen and don't try to block them. Be open to knowledge. Try to learn something new every day.

ROBYN O'BRIEN has been called "food's Erin Brockovich" by the New York Times and Bloomberg. Her story has inspired millions. Robyn was a financial analyst who covered the food industry. She now lends her analytical skill set, heart, and mind to building a better food system.

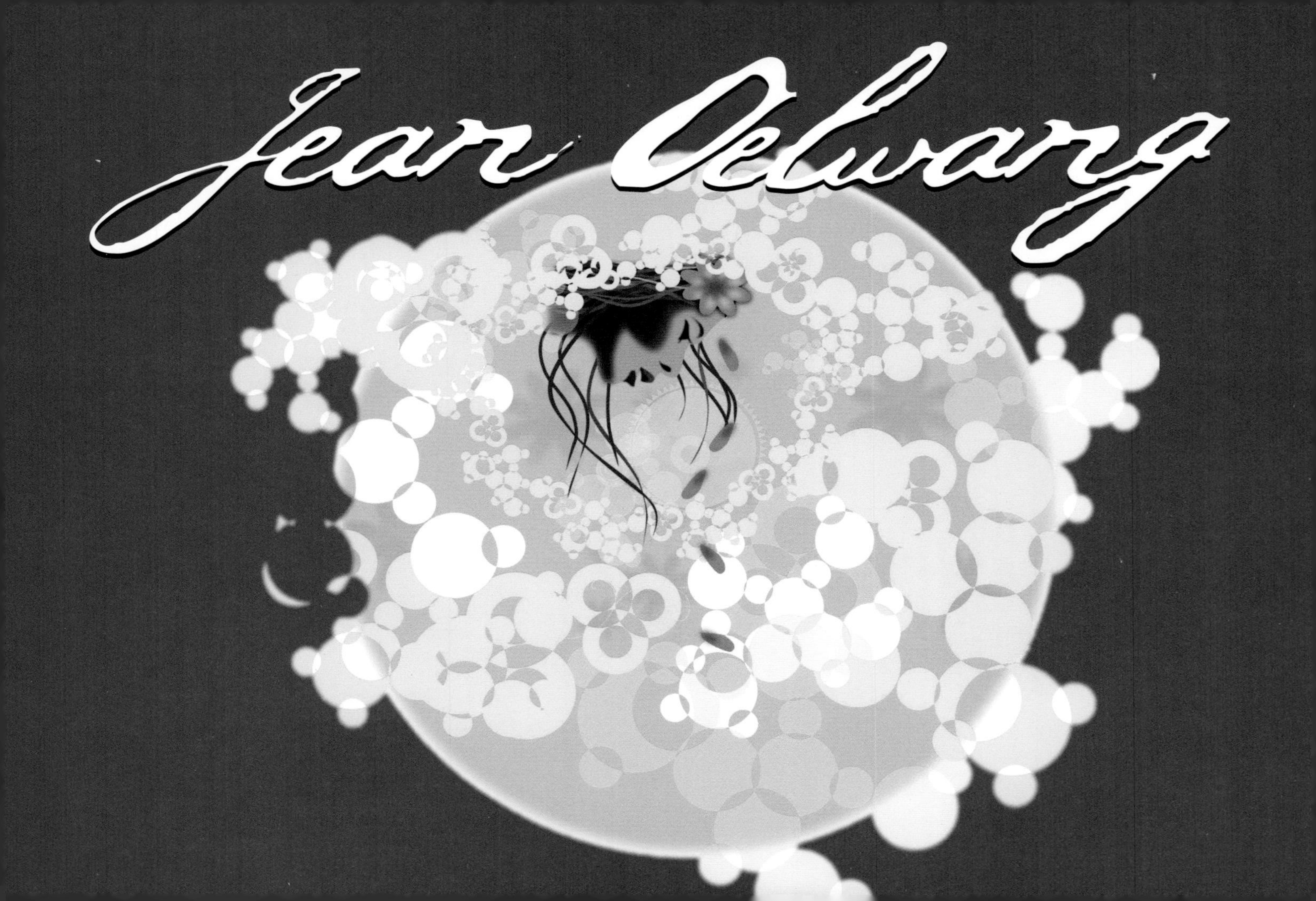
Jean Delvary

What animal or environmental issue gets you out of bed, and why? Ruby, a beautiful red heeler mix, gets me out of bed each morning! What gets me inspired each day is the opportunity to listen and learn from the wonders of Mother Nature. What drives me to act is the Planetary Boundaries work of Johan Rockstrom and a group of scientists. This exciting framing clearly shows the tremendous opportunity humanity has to "stay in Eden" by respecting Mother Nature's boundaries and using innovation and collaboration to deliver abundance for all.

What are you doing about it? The degradation of all major ecosystems, climate change, ocean acidification, and the breaching of other natural boundaries are the greatest challenges and opportunities of our lifetime. We have all the tools we need to reverse course to "stay in Eden." We now need a different operating model, driven by collaboration, compassion, respect for nature, and a sense of urgency. At Virgin Unite, we are working with partners on a number of initiatives including:

- Turning business-as-usual upside down by creating a new economic model that respects, values and celebrates nature in a radically new way; it's a model that includes business leaders listening to and learning from nature's wisdom to re-invent how we live and work in the world.
- Celebrating the ocean as a force that literally keeps us alive by giving us the oxygen we need for every breath.
- Ending our reliance on fossil fuels by supporting the growing movement toward clean energy for all.

What can everyone do about it? What would Mother Nature do? Ask yourself this question and change your relationship with nature in all you do, every day. Stay in Eden! Learn more about the Planetary Boundaries and live in abundance within them. Turn your business upside down to serve people and the planet, rather than the other way around. Listen to one another and to Mother Nature's four billion years of wisdom.

JEAN OELWANG is president and trustee of Virgin Unite, the entrepreneurial foundation of the Virgin Group. She sits on the advisory council for The Elders and the boards of the Carbon War Room, the B Team, Ocean Unite, Ocean Elders, and Just Capital. She worked on five continents helping to lead successful mobile phone start-ups, has hung out with wombats and kangaroos at the Foundation for National Parks and Wildlife in Australia, and did a stint as a VISTA volunteer where she worked with—and learned from—homeless teens in Chicago.

KNOW THAT EACH DECISION DIRECTS OUR FUTURE.

RICHARD PALMQUIST

What animal or environmental issue gets you out of bed, and why? My parents modeled honesty and seeking betterment for others through knowledge well applied. They nurtured my interest in animals, science, and medicine, so it is no surprise that my life ended up dedicated to seeking truth for better healing. My parents also held a deep reverence and awe for spirit and nature. They taught me to love and be truthful so I could best help others. I carry their lessons and work to find a balance in spirit, mind, body, and the relationships associated with life. That goal drives involvement in soils and agriculture, real food nutrition, advancing medical evidence and raising healthy families. It brings me the most fascinating associations.

What are you doing about it? I get up at 5 a.m. to ride my bicycle and watch as my body integrates with the bicycle. I meditate in motion, striving to align divinity and motion for optimal outcomes. I carry that intent through the day with patients in our integrative veterinary practice. Because we love, we touch one another and we seek truth. The search for my truth led me past conventional medicine to find, much to my surprise, that integrative medicine holds entire new vistas of natural healing. I was transformed and feel obligated to help others research this area. I've been mentored by amazing people, lecture at international conferences, teach veterinary students, and instruct professional students in holistic veterinary practice.

What can everyone do about it? We all are born with a song in our hearts, and this aligns with our talents. Finding that song and joining in dialogue and action to manifest our talents in the world is a high calling. Seek truth, learn it, and share it with others. Know that each decision directs our future. If we smile at the world it smiles back, if we do it again, Earth gives us her secrets and all our lives are better for the knowing.

RICHARD PALMQUIST, DVM, grew up in Colorado and graduated from Colorado State University where he was selected as the Upjohn Award recipient for small animal medicine. He is past president and national research chair of the American Holistic Veterinary Medical Foundation where he works to expand research and education in holistic veterinary medicine.

What animal or environmental issue gets you out of bed, and why? The fact that contemporary society takes nature completely for granted disturbs me. We act as if Mother Earth is merely a passive platform that we can use and discard as we fulfill our desire for more and more to consume. It is my deepest desire to reawaken people's consciousness to the fact that nature is, literally, our life support system. When I first stumbled upon America's National Park System with its vast acreage of the scenic, undeveloped lands—the Grand Canyon, Yellowstone, and Yosemite National Parks—I saw that sharing these places could be part of the answer. I believe that the profound impact these places have upon mind, body and soul can have a transformative effect, allowing people to appreciate the natural beauty and value in their own backyards.

What are you doing about it? For twenty years, my husband Frank and I have worked to raise awareness about the National Park System and encourage greater visitation and appreciation, particularly among urban-based people. Many Americans do not know these places exist, and many Americans of color have a troubled history, as these places were once off limits to us. Frank and I have kept a steady stream of information about the parks in the mass media and provided a counterpoint to the long-standing notion that "people of color are not interested in nature and the environment." Given the dire threat of climate change, it's time to get all hands on deck.

What can everyone do about it? The Earth belongs to all of us, and each one of us has a role and responsibility to respect and treat it gently for the benefit of this and future generations. To the extent that each of us holds that sacred trust in our mind, to that extent our involuntary actions will tend to be respectful of the land and of each other.

AUDREY PETERMAN is an environmentalist, writer, and advocate for America's publicly owned lands. She is co-author of Legacy on the Land: A Black Couple Discovers Our National Inheritance and Tells Why Every American Should Care *and author of* Our True Nature: Finding a Zest for Life in the National Park System.

Radhika Srihg

What animal or environmental issue gets you out of bed, and why? I believe that as the advanced species we humans are supposed to protect animals and treasure our world. Instead, we have exploited, overbred, tortured, and wasted many animal lives for little gain. We have broken the circle of life and plundered natural resources. Recalibrating our perceptions of 'progress' so that it takes less of a toll on the natural world is what drives me, while some animals I know inspire me to work a little harder.

What are you doing about it? I am part of a team that uses our voice in media to educate and encourage Sri Lankans to preserve our island's rich biodiversity. We work with expert contributors to communicate issues affecting our wildlife, from respecting our national parks to the escalating elephant-human conflict here. Via the Federation of Environmental Organizations (FEO), I help raise awareness of factors adversely impacting Sri Lanka's natural heritage, including irresposible development. I am also a writer. My first book is an adventure story for young adults and its prevailing theme deals with the spiritual power of animal communication and how little we understand about coexistence.

What can everyone do about it? We are all connected. I encourage people to lean less on mass-market consumerism and focus on supporting local, sustainable initiatives. We are what we eat and so much is wasted while 'Big Business' drives tractors through jungles and keeps animals in deplorable living conditions without dignity in life or death. We can and must co-exist with nature. We must show more empathy toward all animals, not just the ones we like or know. I believe there are more people who care than don't, but the bad guys shout louder right now.

RADHIKA PHILIP, LL.B, Editor of Life Times Sri Lanka *(LT), a monthly magazine. She is a trustee of the FEO in Sri Lanka, who work with interest groups to safeguard Sri Lanka's natural heritage through conservation and advocacy. Radhika's debut novel,* Reyna's Prophecy, *was published in February 2014; she is the first author published and launched from Sri Lanka by the HarperCollins network.*

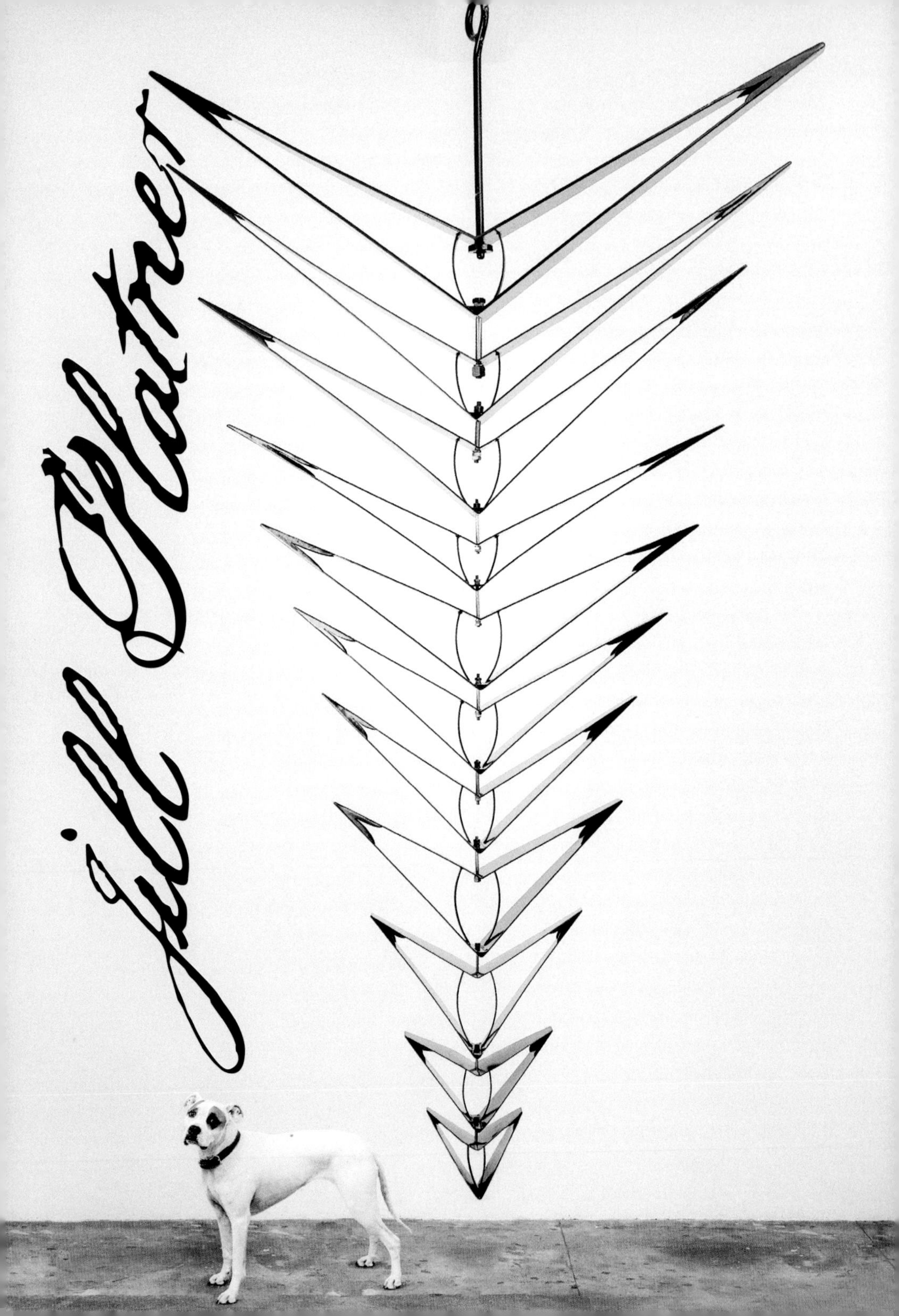
Jill Platner

What animal or environmental issue gets you out of bed, and why? My love for nature moves me. I mean, nature is everything, without it we are nothing! I find ways to connect to nature in an urban environment by creating jewelry and sculpture that celebrates the natural world. As an artist with a small business, I am constantly working to refine our sustainable practices to build a more ethically minded community. If we educate one another, we can all understand that we have the ability to make a huge difference. Contribute each day in a small way, and conserve, preserve, generally create less waste. That's a great start! We are very powerful if we all act together!

What are you doing about it? I love working with metal in general, both precious and non-precious, because it lasts forever, and because I love the process of creating something malleable out of a seemingly hard material. All of my pieces are made by hand—100 percent in New York City, which is a rare happening these days. The jewelry I make is not a fast-fashion business. Each piece is made with care! We have a small production studio and do our very best to maintain sustainable studio practices. All of our metals are recycled. We work with responsibly sourced precious stones and send our metal scraps to be refined and made back into usable silver, gold, and copper. We compost all organic matter at the studio and store and we teach our staff about our practices and provide them with their own reusable totes to reduce the habit of carrying plastic bags.

What can everyone do about it? I think when buying jewelry (or anything for that matter!) it's important to consider how and where it's produced as well as the origin of the materials. It's definitely always an added bonus if its recycled, recyclable, locally made or grown, but thinking about whether or not the company engages in any kind of eco-activity and concern for the environment is always key. We need to stop buying disposable items and make smarter, ethical purchases. If you buy quality, it lasts a lifetime!

*For more than twenty years, **JILL PLATNER** has created jewelry and sculpture. Since 1993, her work has been sold worldwide. For Jill, no matter what the scale of the work, the process remains an intimate one. Every piece, large or small, is hand made locally with a keen eye to detail, ensuring the highest level of quality and the singular passion for craftsmanship for which Jill is known.*

Jasmine Solsvorelli

What animal or environmental issue gets you out of bed, and why? Fur trapping. Trapping innocent animals is inhumane and unnecessary. Trapping has nothing to do with conservation, nuisance control, or tradition; it's about greed and vanity. Twelve-year-olds can possess a trapper's license. Kids are taught to take a life when they should be taught to respect life. In Canada, large-name manufacturers use fur trim on their outerwear and claim it is needed for our harsh winters. These jackets are purchased by people who are drawn to brand names; it has nothing to do with staying warm, it's all about belonging to a vain club. How can holding an animal against its will, taking its life, and stripping it of its skin be considered a humane practice?

What are you doing about it? To help end fur trapping, I work to raise awareness by speaking to consumers at anti-fur demos. Many people are unaware of what an animal must go through for people to wear outerwear with fur trim or a fur coat. Our demos have been very successful changing peoples' minds—many returning fur jackets they've purchased and some even joining us at the demos. In interviews, I speak about trapping from the animals' perspective and discuss the real reasons animals are trapped. I support anti-fur campaigns and belong to organizations that are active in putting an end to this inhumane practice.

What can everyone do about it? Don't purchase any products that contain fur. Don't fall for propaganda from organizations that benefit directly from the purchase of those fur products. Educate yourself through proper resources and speak up for exploited and innocent animals. Support campaigns that work to end fur trapping. Participate in anti-fur demonstrations and help educate people on the real price behind fur. Don't be afraid to share what you've learned, even if you must stand alone. The animals need your voice.

JASMINE is a passionate animal advocate committed to speaking up for those who cannot speak for themselves. Raised in a vegan family, she learned from an early age that her voice was the greatest tool she could use to change the world for the better. Though her commitment to animal rights has a broad platform, currently her primary focus is raising awareness about the inhumane practice of wildlife trapping and helping to run an authorized wildlife rehabilitation center located in Ontario, Canada. She's 13 years old.

Alison Pouliot

What animal or environmental issue gets you out of bed, and why? Getting out of bed is not an issue – life is short and there's so much nature to experience! But so much is also disappearing. While the so-called charismatic megafauna need attention, the more obscure, unseen or disregarded organisms commonly slip through the cracks of conservation. I try to illuminate the curiosities and ecological significance of the fungus kingdom and draw attention to its conservation.

What are you doing about it? I try to inspire an environmental ethic. There's no point in telling people to care. Imposed moral imperatives of conservation can be counterproductive. People need to work it out for themselves, feel it for themselves, and I think that requires being there. I'm simply trying to vitalize the process by encouraging direct and sensory engagement with fungi and with all of nature. Historically fungi have not always been regarded kindly. I guess I'm trying to put to rest the fears and misconceptions about fungi and encourage other ways of thinking, sensing, and feeling about these organisms. And rally for their inclusion in biodiversity conservation. Recognizing the role of fungi in terrestrial ecosystems, and valuing them for their aesthetics and extraordinariness seems like a good place to begin. I guess it's also about my own interest in visually documenting fungi in all their peculiarities.

What can everyone do about it? Go bush! Get out in it. Revisit the real world. Meet some fungi. Many fungi appear in autumn and what better way to enjoy the sensuality and introspection of this season than a forest stroll engaging with fungi? There are practical things we can do to maximize the chance of their (and hence our) continued existence. Mostly it's about maintaining habitat – not compromising it, spraying chemicals on it, fragmenting it, compacting it, or polluting it. It's about realizing that fungi live in intimate association with other organisms. Perhaps most important, it's about recognizing our own inherent connectedness with and dependence on these organisms. It's about forming a peace contract.

ALISON POULIOT is an ecologist and environmental photographer. Her work documents biodiversity and environmental change in images and words. Alison runs fungus forays in Australia and Europe to introduce people to the fungus kingdom.

Vapre Fately

Coal Seam Gas Fields.

What animal or environmental issue gets you out of bed, and why? Coal seam gas and the unconventional gas industry get me out of bed. The industry treads on people's basic rights: it's taking over farms; it's taking over our environment. The destruction is long-term and the people making money from it are going to take their bags of gold and leave us with a toxic mess. I'm not prepared to stand by and let that happen. I believe in a fair go for everybody, including our future generations. We cannot use resources like we are now and expect there will be no repercussions down the line.

What are you doing about it? I'm a landholder and I helped make a film called Frackman about my battle with the unconventional gas industry. I've spent years blockading and protesting, and I now lecture across the country. I've come to realize that banking supports this industry activity. I'm trying to take money away from unethical companies by letting people know that we have other banking options and we can vote on what we feel is important with our dollar. If our money is going to fund something, let it be something that doesn't destroy us. I want the industry to understand that we are serious about protecting our homes and that we will not be bullied—and that's where divestment comes in.

What can everyone do about it? If we do not stand up as a group and ask our leaders—and ourselves—to do better, we'll be run by corporate interests. Choose wisely what you do with your money, where and how you spend your money, and consume less. Reuse, recycle, and love what you've got and stop looking for the next best thing; the best thing you've got is *now*. Embrace it, live it, and love it. You might come to a new place in your life and you'll find people that you didn't know before. That's what I've done and life couldn't be better. Really, life couldn't be better.

DAYNE PRATZKY is the subject of the 2015 documentary Frackman, *which chronicles his efforts to protect his home and health from the coal seam gas industry in Queensland, Australia. Dayne travels the world sharing his story, offering practical advice about standing up to big industry and inspiring others to stand up in their community by becoming their own heroes. Dayne has battled the industry for six years and has faced many setbacks in his journey, but he maintains there is a good reason to get up in the morning: coffee.*

What animal or environmental issue gets you out of bed, and why? There have been the five major extinctions in the history of the planet and we're going through a sixth right now. There are multiple drivers to early extinction but the scary thing is that it's all human – it's all human-caused, it's all anthropogenic. *Racing extinction* it's what gets me out of bed and keeps me out of it.

What are you doing about it? Films, to me, are a very powerful tool. I call them my "weapon of mass construction." Someone drops a "bomb," it kills something. I make a film about it, I create allies, and things change. That's what I do every day. My first film was *The Cove*, an Oscar-winning documentary about the slaughter of dolphins. *The Cove* has been seen by millions, but most important, it's helped cut the slaughter of dolphins to about a third of what it was. In my new project, *Racing Extinction*, we track Shawn Heinrichs and Paul Hilton as they work to get the manta ray listed as an endangered species under the Convention on International Trade for Endangered Species (CITES). Because of their efforts, Indonesia, which once killed mantas at a horrifying rate, is now one of the world's most significant manta sanctuaries. Those two men accomplished this in the four-year span of this movie.

What can everyone do about it? Margaret Mead, the anthropologist, said, "Never doubt that a few thoughtful citizens can change the world, indeed it's the only thing that ever has…" and we show that in *Racing Extinction*. You see these people do amazing things. It pulls the rug out of the "Oh, what can I do? I'm just one person," argument. If we all do a small thing (or several) – become a vegan, ride your bike to work, turn off the lights, then everyone has a chance to become a superhero. I mean in 1995, people were saying we'd never get cigarettes off planes, there are too many smokers, the airline industry won't have it, and now it's illegal I think on every airline in the world.

*The executive director of the Oceanic Preservation Society, **LOUIE PSIHOYOS** is widely regarded as one of the world's most preeminent still photographers. He has circled the globe dozens of times photographing people and places for the world's most highly regarded magazines including* National Geographic, Smithsonian, Discover, Time, Newsweek, *the* New York Times Magazine, Sports Illustrated *and many others. His imagination, wit, and iconic imagery have helped illustrate a wide array of*

Malcolm Kards

What animal or environmental issue gets you out of bed, and why? "We don't know what we don't know" about laundry detergent. We know what we like—it works, it's economical, it smells good, it's easy to use. But if I were to ask most people what's in the laundry detergent, they wouldn't be able to tell me. At last count, there were more than 84,000 chemicals available for commercial use around the world, with 1,000 new chemicals introduced every year. Regulation hasn't been able to keep up with chemical development. Long after these chemicals have been approved for everyday use, we find links between some of these chemicals and health concerns—hormone disruption, allergies, asthma, and even cancer. And in nearly all countries, cleaning product manufacturers are not required to list ingredients on their packaging, which perpetuates the idea that consumers don't really need to know. But we do list every ingredient. We need to challenge basic assumptions about the products in our homes.

What are you doing about it? I work to raise awareness of the nasty chemicals used in everyday household products, from laundry detergent to baby products, and offer safer alternatives. My partner Melanie and I started *ecostore* in 1993 to provide safe, sustainable alternatives to synthetic chemicals at competitive prices. Our plant- and mineral-based products do the same hard work as the cheapest and harshest chemicals in commercial use today. Our entire production process is eco-friendly—from products to the packaging.

What can everyone do about it? Ask questions and find brands you can trust. Look for and demand transparency. Everyone has a right to know what's in the products they are using on themselves and on the most vulnerable people in their households—their babies and small children. If you're not sure about the safety of an ingredient, use online resources like the Environmental Working Group's (EWG) Cosmetic Database. It offers a comprehensive list of chemical ingredients with an easy-to-follow safety rating, or contact the manufacturer directly.

*MALCOLM and **MELANIE RANDS** started ecostore to develop and market healthier, eco-friendlier household cleaners, body care, and baby products with a focus on looking after the health and well-being of people as well as the planet. ecostore's team of chemists continually reviews and refines product formulations as new science changes what we know.*

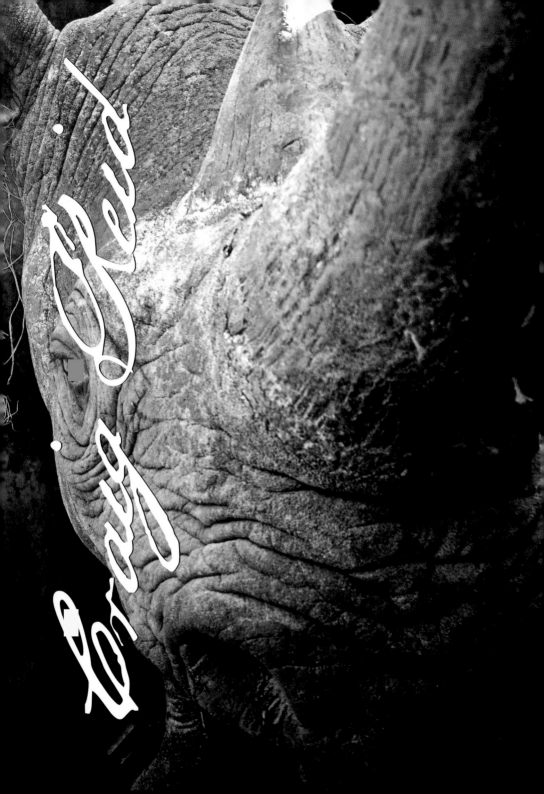

What animal or environmental issue gets you out of bed, and why? It would be great to spring out of bed, swirl into a phone booth, and emerge as a conservation superhero able to resolve the multitude of environmental crises that beset our planet. Sadly and far more sobering, the real solutions depend on everyday people who commit long term to manage African Protected Areas. I know that through grim determination and attending to the often-less-than-exciting tasks, I will contribute to their sustainable long-term success. These places are the last refuges for many species of wildlife. I wake up daily for them.

What are you doing about it? I have been actively involved in the hands-on field management and administration of Protected Areas in Africa. In my earlier years, I had plenty of time in the trenches on patrol with game scouts directly ensuring the security of species under threat, including white and black rhinos. I have always had an open mind and have never been afraid to try new initiatives. This has resulted in some fantastic projects such as extending the range of endangered species, working to protect the African wild dogs, and the reestablishment of species hunted to extinction. I am privileged to work for a great African conservation organization, African Parks Network.

What can everyone do about it? You ask, "What difference will my small action make?" Too often, this leads to inaction. Results can only come from action and every small action counts. Know that as conservation-minded people, we belong to a tribe of determined individuals that have made significant changes. Whenever you feel hopeless, know that somewhere someone is lying in an ambush risking his or her life on the frontline of conservation, and somewhere else, others may be helping breeding frogs cross a busy highway. We all have our role to play. Make something happen, and be a part of the solution now. We need resources to keep the last remaining areas intact, please help us, and remain positive. I am terminally optimistic—it may kill me one day, but I am enjoying the process!

*For more than 23 years, **CRAIG REID** has served as an African Protected Area manager, pilot, wilderness guide, and terminal optimist in a range of wild African places.*

What animal or environmental issue gets you out of bed, and why? Children, animals, the elderly, and the environment top my list of concerns. The first three are affected by the fourth, whether it's renewable energy, responsible farming, thoughtful urban development or the care and nurturing of our natural resources. I am a big fan of Community Supported Agriculture (CSA) and I'm pleased that it's becoming more accessible in urban and sub-urban areas and more widely integrated in the public school system. My biggest concern with regard to responsible farming is hydro-fracking and its irreversible and damaging impacts on the environment, and the widespread use of GMOs.

What are you doing about it? I buy a good portion of produce from local farmers for use in my business and have offered cooking sessions with the area's CSAs focusing on seasonal ingredients and simple techniques. I talk about cooking and using fresh, local, seasonal ingredients to anyone who will listen. I would like, in the near future, to develop a public school–based food initiative that involves students in the entire process of farming, seed harvesting, canning, and cooking. People make a big deal about how much time it takes to shop for and cook our foods and this aversion is encouraged by the fast food industry and middlemen who do everything from telling us what to eat to choosing it for us. I am involved with a New York-based group to ban hydro-fracking and gas pipeline construction especially when eminent domain is used to force property owners to forfeit their land for financial gain in the corporate/private sector.

What can everyone do about it? Make an effort to be more informed—and inform our children—about where food comes from, what we eat, and how we prepare and consume our food. Take responsibility for food we waste, eliminate processed foods from your diet, and try to be self-sufficient. Also, remember that the process of preparing, sharing, and eating food is an intimate one. Taking the time to cook a meal gives us a direct relationship with what we put into our bodies and deepens the relationships with people with whom we share our food.

DELISSA REYNOLDS is a New York-based actor and celebrated neighborhood activist, bar owner and food enthusiast. In 2004, she opened the neighborhood hub Bar Sepia and is developing her podcast cooking show and cookbook series Chef In A Shoebox: Big Meals From Small Spaces. She is a recipient of the Eileen Fisher Women In Business Grant, the Eileen Fisher "Take Part: In Her Company Campaign" and The NYC Small Business Neighborhood Achievement Award.

What animal or environmental issue gets you out of bed, and why? The biggest environmental issue we all face is the continued overuse by human beings of our planet's limited resources. That is what's behind climate change, freshwater scarcity, extinction of species, deforestation, desertification...the list goes on, and it's getting worse because all of us are consuming more at the same time our population is growing more. These two things combined have created an annual compounded growth of the global economy that is overriding the benefits from all our sustainability innovations combined.

What are you doing about it? At Patagonia, we challenge our customers to reduce their personal consumption—including not buying our stuff if they don't really need it. We launched the effort in 2012 with a full-page ad in the New York Times featuring a photo of our best-selling jacket and the headline "Don't Buy This Jacket." In the ad, we explained that in spite of our efforts to make the jacket with no unnecessary harm to the environment, it still had a significant environmental footprint: 135 liters of water, 20 pounds of CO_2 emissions, 24 times its weight in waste. We continue to use print and digital media to bring awareness to this issue so that all of us—our company and our customers—can be part of the solution instead of the problem.

What can everyone do about it? Buy only what we need, and when we do need it, select products that are durable and well made. The most effective way to reduce the environmental impact of a product is to use for a long time. Fix it if it's broken, give, or sell it to someone else if you're not using it, and recycle it when it's truly worn out. Through our Worn Wear initiative, we encourage our customers to repair, resell, and recycle. It's responsible consumption, and we consider ourselves in the business of providing responsible products to people that want to live responsible lives.

RICK RIDGEWAY is Patagonia's vice president of environmental affairs. Guided by the company's mission statement: Build the best product, cause no unnecessary harm, use business to inspire and implement solutions to the environmental crisis, Rick has led vanguard environmental and sustainability initiatives including Freedom to Roam, Common Threads and the Footprint Chronicles. He co-founded the Sustainable Apparel Coalition (SAC). Rick is one of the world's foremost mountaineers and adventurers, a filmmaker and a writer. National Geographic recently honored him with its "Lifetime Achievement in Adventure" award. Rick lives with his wife in Ojai, California, and they have three grown children.

BE AWARE.

BE CURIOUS.

Find your passion,

be involved!

Nancy Rosenthal

What animal or environmental issue gets you out of bed, and why? Coral reefs, big fish, big cats, biodiversity, global warming, illegal animal trafficking, habitats—the many things that are threatened yet so vital to life on this earth get me going! We need the oceans, elephants, and trees. It's all critical to our survival and to the survival of future generations. And it's up to us. I wake up in the morning ready to use the most powerful tool I know—film—to change people's attitudes about their own role in protecting the environment.

What are you doing about it? My work as a producer at National Geographic opened my eyes to the positive impact of film. Because so many films speak to the heart of an environmental issue, energize us about the magnificence of the outdoors, tell stories of hope and survival, and inspire people to take action, I created a platform to share these powerful films with live audiences. The New York WILD Film Festival showcases films about exploration, adventure, wildlife, conservation, and the environment. When you add to the film screenings a lively dialog among the filmmakers, scientists, explorers, and a New York audience, a community evolves that shares ideas and strategies for real change. Richard Zimmerman, founder of Orangutan Outreach, joined a panel at the 2011 festival for a screening of the film, Green. The film is an emotional journey across Indonesia showing the devastating impact of deforestation and resource exploitation on orangutans. After the program and panel discussion, several people were so moved by the film that they vowed not to purchase items made with tropical wood and palm oil. Others donated funding to Richard's organization and other great ape conservation efforts.

What can everyone do about it? Be aware. Be curious. Find your passion, be involved! Explore the world, especially through film and through your own adventures. Learn more. Once you have a better understanding of the issues facing the environment, act to protect what you value most. If one person sees a film and shares what they learned with their children or a friend, or if they eat sustainable seafood for a healthy ocean, or reduce plastic use, the festival has accomplished something. The small actions do count! Celebrate the Wild.

NANCY ROSENTHAL is the founder and executive director of the New York WILD Film Festival.

What animal or environmental issue gets you out of bed, and why? Our oceans. They provide half of all the oxygen we breathe and are the main source of protein for billions of people around the world, yet we discard anything we don't want—from trash and toxic pollutants to tons of plastic—into our oceans. More than half of the 300 million tons of plastic we produce every year is used once and thrown away, but with plastic, there really is no "away". Plastic isn't disposable, plastic is *indestructible*. (How did we ever believe we could just throw it "away"? It seems obvious, but many things we use now seem crazy to me.) Most people don't even think about the fact that plastic comes from oil—and we all know that our precious oil reserves will not last forever. Let's end this addiction we have to single-use plastic.

What are you doing about it? I focus on how plastic waste impacts the ocean, enters the food chain, and effects human health. I am producing a documentary feature film, *Plastic Oceans* (working title), and co-founded the Plastic Oceans Foundation to raise the funds we need to complete the film. We are developing education, science and policy, and business and sustainability programs and are continuing to raise funds for research and campaigns. I give presentations to schools and the public—I talk about it to anyone who might listen. Once people understand the issue, something changes in their psyche and they start to look at things differently. I believe we can solve the problem within a generation if we put our minds to it.

What can everyone do about it? First, remember that plastic isn't disposable, it's indestructible. Then make simple changes: don't accept plastic bags and refuse drinking straws; use wooden matches instead of disposable plastic lighters; drink tap water; stop using body scrubs made with plastic microbeads; choose fruits and vegetables that are not wrapped in plastic; wash up after a picnic; and take your own plates and cutlery. Consider how much plastic you throw away each week and how you can reduce your plastic footprint. Recycle any plastic that cannot be re-used.

JO RUXTON is a co-founder the Plastic Oceans Foundation (POF), has produced the Plastic Oceans documentary feature and also leads the foundation›s conservation and education programs. She has worked on underwater wildlife documentaries for the BBC Natural History Unit and is the former World Wide Fund for Nature head of conservation in Hong Kong where she established their marine conservation program.

IT IS HIGH TIME
FOR HUMANITY
TO GROW UP
INTO ITS
EVOLUTIONARY
MATURITY.

Elisabet Sahtouris

What animal or environmental issue gets you out of bed, and why? We have brought the perfect storm of crises in ecology, economy, and society on ourselves. It looks overwhelming to many people, but for me – and many others – it is an enormously exciting opportunity to change the way we live on Earth and live with each other. That's what gets me out of bed each day! It makes my blood rush to envision an inspired, enthusiastic humanity learning to live in clean, green ways and in cooperative harmony with all our fellow Earth beings.

What are you doing about it? My deep study of evolutionary biology revealed an evolutionary maturation cycle from competition to cooperation that all surviving, thriving species go through. Feisty and even hostile competition is a youthful phase that species outgrow (often in times of crises when hostilities become far more costly than cooperation). Aware that science has only given us a Darwinian story for the youthful competitive phase of this cycle, I call for an equally inspiring story about the ecstasy of forming a mature, peaceful, harmonious, cooperative community worldwide. It is high time for humanity to grow up into its evolutionary maturity.

What can everyone do about it? All my thinking, writing, speaking and teaching is aimed at getting as many people as possible to begin living the future NOW. The future is not something to sit and wait for, but for us to co-create actively. If we treat each other now the way we want people to treat each other, feed and nurture our bodies in ways we'd like everyone to do, seek out clean green energy and elegantly simple lifestyles, participate in the wellbeing of our families and communities with the kind of love and generosity we'd like to see everywhere in the future, then all this will *become* our future.

ELISABET SAHTOURIS, Ph.D., is an internationally recognized evolution biologist, futurist, author, lecturer and consultant. She brings principles of living systems into the corporate world, governments and other organizations. A professor who has lived in the USA, Canada, Greece, Peru and Spain, she taught at MIT and the University of Massachusetts, contributed to the NOVA/HORIZON series at WGBH-TV Boston and has been a UN consultant on indigenous peoples. She holds a Chair in Living Economies at the World Business Academy and is currently a professor at Chaminade University in Hawaii. Her books include EarthDance: Living Systems in Evolution, Biology Revisioned, a dialog with Willis Harman; A Walk Through Time: From Stardust to Us; and Gaia's Dance: The Story of Earth & Us.

What animal or environmental issue gets you out of bed, and why? Resilience in nature: the power of nature to bounce back if humans allow for it. Many times I have been struck by how fast plants and animals can recolonize areas and how nature takes its course if we let go. Like along Dutch rivers that were given more freedom by removing dikes or lowering flood plains. At a larger scale, Europe is witnessing a spectacular comeback of iconic wildlife species like the grey wolf, beaver, red deer, bison, seals, eagles, vultures, storks and cranes. This gives me hope—it does not only show that conservation works, it is also indicates the huge potential for rewilding!

What are you doing about it? In 2011 I co-founded Rewilding Europe, an initiative that uses a historic opportunity to advocate a vision for a wilder continent, with much more space for natural processes, wild nature and wildlife – where local communities benefit through new, nature-based activities. Ten large landscapes across the continent are on their way to becoming inspirational showcases of this vision – apart from many other smaller examples. Rewilding Europe invites and works with landowners, local communities, park managers, hunting associations, business people, fellow conservationists, local and national governments, financial partners and many others to make this a reality.

What can everyone do about it? Rewilding is a new appreciation of wild nature – it starts in our minds and requires a different attitude – letting nature do much more of its own job instead of actively managing and controlling it. There is a lot of potential for rewilding – in Europe nearly 18 percent of the land surface is under some form of conservation status. Also, there is a substantial land abandonment happening across many regions – and as more people live in urban areas they like to go out to experience wild nature and wildlife. This provides completely new economic opportunities for rural communities. Rewilding can be applied to any place, at any scale – from your own garden into the larger landscapes. Start rewilding and be surprised and inspired how nature will respond!

FRANS SCHEPERS (The Netherlands) is Managing Director of Rewilding Europe. He graduated in forestry, land, and water management in 1985 after which he took various positions in nature conservation. From 2000–2014, he worked for the World Wide Fund for Nature on international programs on species conservation, ecological networks and freshwater programs, in particular in Southern Africa, Europe and Eurasia. During his professional career, which now spans over twenty-five years, he specialized in developing conservation strategies, protected area management and financing, species conservation, establishing ecological networks and rewilding approaches.

Alokparna Sergayha

What animal or environmental issue gets you out of bed, and why? I am particularly passionate about the plight of more than 100 million animals used for scientific experimentation – whether it is basic research into biology, assessing new medicines, or testing consumer products such as cosmetics, household cleaners, food additives, and agro-chemicals. Compassionate, thinking citizens condemn any other form of animal cruelty but experimentation on animals is often assumed unavoidable and important for the greater good and human health. The harm inflicted on these animals is unthinkable, and the research is often unreliable. People tolerate the suffering because they think it benefits humans, but much of the science is outdated. This is a motivating challenge for me. We exploit animals in so many ways and the desire – and opportunity – to stop this gets me out of bed every day.

What are you doing about it? I work with the world's largest animal protection organization, Humane Society International (HSI), to end animal testing. We run the #BeCrueltyFree campaign, the world's largest campaign to end animal testing for cosmetics, including sunscreen, creams, shampoo, deodorants, and so on. We persuaded the Indian government and industry to ban animal testing for cosmetics and prohibit the import of animal-tested cosmetics into our country. It is an important first step. We are now working with scientists to refine, reduce, and replace animal testing wherever applicable. We also work with the government to divert funds away from unsatisfactory animal testing and toward development of state-of-the-art in vitro, computational, and robotic tools to test for and make predictions regarding real-world risks to people.

What can everyone do about it? You can help by choosing to shop cruelty-free. Visit the leapingbunny website to know which cosmetics are not tested on animals or, if in the store, look for the leaping bunny logo. Sign the #BeCrueltyFree pledge to support a ban on animal testing for cosmetics around the world. Contact your favorite brands, ask if their products are cruelty free and if not, and urge them to make the leap. Write to your legislators and tell them to fund alternatives to animal testing. If you pursue a career in science and research, choose a field that doesn't exploit animals, but develops cutting-edge alternatives instead. Every little step anyone makes toward this will make a real difference.

ALOKPARNA SENGUPTA, M.SC, is the deputy director for Humane Society International/ India and the campaign manager for Be Cruelty-Free, India. Before joining Humane Society International, she worked at Thomson Reuters in Hyderabad, India as a patent analyst.

What animal or environmental issue gets you out of bed, and why? I have been privileged by circumstance to share my entire life with African elephants. They—and their wondrous ways – have been a part of my life since the moment I took my first steps in Kenya's magnificent Tsavo National Park. Growing up, I could never have imagined a planet without them, but today, we are faced with that very real possibility. I am committed to halting this madness.

What are you doing about it? With The David Sheldrick Wildlife Trust team, I rear orphaned elephants, the youngest victims of the ivory trade, steering them through infancy and adolescence into adulthood, and ultimately returning them back to the wild where they rightly belong. This has come with both great joy and a good dose of heartache too. Every one of them has left an indelible imprint on my heart and filled me with wonder and awe. We fight on the front lines operating anti-poaching teams and mobile veterinary units. We witness the price paid every day by an African elephant so that someone a world away can own an ornament carved from an ivory tooth.

What can everyone do about it? Nature is essential to the well-being of the Earth as a whole. It is the balm of the human spirit and we – as the dominant species – have an obligation to nurture and protect nature rather than desecrate and destroy it. We can live without owning ivory. Choose to be part of the solution rather than the cause.

ANGELA SHELDRICK is the CEO of The David Sheldrick Wildlife Trust. The David Sheldrick Wildlife Trust is a registered charity in Kenya dedicated to the protection and conservation of wildlife and habitats.

What animal or environmental issue gets you out of bed, and why? The urgent need for environmental justice. Many communities of color, low-income, and indigenous people live in areas where they cannot breathe clean air, drink clean water, go to safe schools, live in a toxin-free home, or have access to healthy food. Exposure to pollutants and toxins scar the health and landscapes of America— from Alaska to the Gulf Coast, from tribal lands to urban areas – and contribute to our declining health and poor birth outcomes. It's an intergenerational problem.

What are you doing about it? I founded a nonprofit, WE ACT, to expand democratic space for the people and perspectives of affected communities to be heard and incorporated into solutions. Through community organizing, policy reform and community-based participatory research, we engage residentsfortified with data, confidence and a vision of community sustainability—in community-based planning to affect political decision making. WE ACT's work has contributed to city, state and federal policy on diesel retrofits, air quality regulations, pesticides, chemicals such as BPA and flame retardants, climate change and environmental justice.

What can everyone do about it? We need collective action by affected residents and diverse stakeholders to help create the change we all need. We must get out of our silos and understand that creating healthy sustainable communities means that those of us who are in education, health, transportation, housing, philanthropy, economic development, technology, and industry, can collaborate to mobilize the will and existing resources to support, develop and implement effective climate, energy, and environmental policies that sustain our health, economy and environment.

PEGGY SHEPARD, co-founder and executive director of West Harlem Environmental Action (WE ACT), has effectively combined grassroots organizing, environmental advocacy, and community-based participatory research to become a national leader in advancing environmental policy and the perspective of environmental justice in urban communities—to ensure that the right to a clean, healthy, and sustainable environment extends to all. She has received the Heinz Award for the Environment, Jane Jacobs Medal for Lifetime Leadership from Rockefeller Foundation, Rachel Carson Award from Audubon, an Honorary Doctor of Science from Smith College, and the Calver Award from the American Public Health Association.

What animal or environmental issue gets you out of bed, and why? Factory farming—the mass production of animals for food—is responsible for extraordinary animal abuses. It appalls me. Within factory farms, pregnant pigs are caged indoors in crates of steel and cement for the bulk of their productive lives, battery hens are locked in cages and unable to properly stretch their wings, and super-sized meat chickens are crammed with tens of thousands of others into giant sheds. None of these sentient beings will ever feel as much as a blade of grass under their feet. To me, this is abuse on an industrial scale. More than 500 million animals in Australia alone are suffering for the food industry.

What are you doing about it? In 2004, my daughter Ondine and I founded Voiceless, the animal protection institute, to lift the veil of secrecy about what goes on in Australia's factory farms. Voiceless spreads the animal protection message, brings the institutionalized suffering of animals to the forefront of Australia's agenda and works to establish animal protection as the next great social justice movement. Voiceless has supported the publication of the first animal law textbooks in Australian history, helped establish animal law as a discipline in many of Australia's universities, and created an annual Voiceless Animal Law Lecture Series to bring the world's most prominent and successful international animal law experts to Australia. Voiceless also offers financial assistance to animal organizations through our grants program and created the Voiceless Media Prizes, encouraging journalists to pursue animal protection stories and build broad public education on animal issues.

What can everyone do about it? Individuals need to understand the truth behind their forks, to learn about the cruelty within factory farming. Consumers have a great deal of power and influence over what practices and industries society will tolerate. It is important for people to change their perception of food to one that reflects reality, to understand that a chicken leg is actually a chicken's leg.

BRIAN SHERMAN, AM Hon Litt D (UTS), is the cofounder and joint managing director of Voiceless, the animal protection institute. Before turning his attention to animal protection, Brian served as the chairman, president, or director of a number of investment companies and nonprofit entities.

NEVER LOOK AWAY

WHEN YOU SEE SOMETHING YOU KNOW IS WRONG, SAY AND DO SOMETHING ABOUT IT

Jennifer Skiff

What animal or environmental issue gets you out of bed, and why? Factory farming, chemical testing, poaching species to extinction, trophy hunting, and puppy farming are just a few of the injustices perpetrated against the helpless that get me out of bed every morning because I know that with others, I can make a difference

What are you doing about it? In 1997, while visiting the country of Laos, I witnessed horrific abuse against sun and moon bears. Five were on display at a park and had literally grown into their cages. My boyfriend told me not to look. He said there was nothing I could do about it. I walked up to one of the bears and he reached for me, pleading for help. My eyes shifted from his teary eyes to his blistered paws. I asked an attendant what was wrong and he said people put cigarettes out on them. At that moment, I vowed I would never look away. It took three years, but working with the communist government, raising money with friends, and enlisting the help of the World Society for the Protection of Animals, I secured the bears' release and built a sanctuary for them. It was worth it! Two years ago, in the garden of a hotel in Indonesia, I witnessed a similar situation with chained and neglected monkeys. This time, I wasn't alone in my objection. Others had been outraged before me. Because of their voices and my intervention, the hotel was prepared to end the nightmare. Working with the hotel's manager, 12 monkeys were released to their original home in the jungle. Sadly, the exploitation of animals goes on all around us. So I work with charities around the world and write books to help create change. My motto remains: *Never look away.*

What can everyone do about it? When you see something you know is wrong, say and do something about it. Your voice matters. Ask your government representatives to support laws that protect animals. Sign petitions. Don't look away.

JENNIFER SKIFF is an animal advocate, an award-winning journalist, and the bestselling author of God Stories *and* The Divinity of Dogs. *She is a Trustee of the Dogs' Refuge Home and SPCA of Hancock County and is the Chair of the Humane Society of the United States Maine State Council. With her favorite Aussie and beloved rescue dogs, Jennifer spends her life in perpetual summer between Maine, USA and Australia.*

WE NEED A REVOLUTION!

HOLLEY SOMERVILLE-KNOTT

Holley Somerville-Knott

What animal or environmental issue gets you out of bed, and why? Our planet is in crisis. Animal welfare, deforestation, ocean acidification, pollution, factory farming, homelessness, poverty, inequality, renewable energy sources, live exports, human rights, climate change, wildlife protection, unconventional gas mining and fracking are all issues I care about. They call for us to choose love, unite together, and co-create a peaceful and sustainable Mother Earth. It's time for governments, investors, corporations, and citizens to work together to develop and deliver low-carbon, humane technologies, which can sustain growth within our planet's and species' boundaries, while creating new opportunities for investment, growth and employment.

What are you doing about it? I started Stardust Foundation, a charity, when I was 8 years old. I sing to raise money and awareness on important issues, then donate it to people and organizations who are caring about our planet and its species. I also speak at schools and events, sing at festivals, and speak at protests and campaigns. I will also be launching the Global Care Project to inspire other kids and people to care. It's an exciting initiative across three key areas—care about the planet, care about yourself, care about each other.

What can everyone do about it? We need a revolution! A green revolution! Green is the new black, yo! Join my Global Care Project or join other groups who are doing something about issues that matter to you. Stop using plastic and chemicals. Grow your own food and create natural areas. Buy from local markets. Choose not to buy anything with palm oil, that comes from animals, or has been tested on animals. We are all part of one big ecosystem, and need to support each other—all species deserve life. Be informed and proactive.

HOLLEY SOMERVILLE-KNOTT is the 11-year-old CEO and founder of the Stardust Foundation. She is an award-winning speaker, activist, and peacemaker. She is a United Nations partner who cares deeply about the planet and all species. Holley's mission is to spread kindness and compassion, and to educate and inspire people to stand up for what they believe in, unite together, and co-create a sustainable and peaceful Mother Earth. Holley has worked with many organizations, including the United Nations Association, HBO New York, Uplift Connect, Drop4drop UK, and Earth Guardians Colorado. She has been a contestant on "The Voice" TV show, and has been touring the jazz/blues circuit this year. She is the winner of the 2014 Youth Sustainability Champion. Holly is also planning a web series/talk TV show to raise awareness on social justice and environmental issues.

Madison Stewart

Good youth, in a bad sea.

What animal or environmental issue gets you out of bed, and why? Sharks. I spent my childhood with sharks and consider them nothing short of family. Their presence in my life emphasizes the most important part of my personality—the part that wants to be different and challenge our ways in society. When I was a teenager, I noticed a rapid decline in the species on the Great Barrier Reef. Seeing such a change worried me and I became an advocate for the species. I want the species to be protected and I fight for them the way any good person fights for what they believe in.

What are you doing about it? When the government failed to listen, I took the fight to the people, targeting the trade consumers, corporations and fishing industries responsible for the unjustified and inhumane killing and decimation of sharks. I have been successful pinpointing and exposing their flaws. I make films about sharks. I pour my heart into these small, simple films that so that people can see and change their perception of sharks. Without a love or respect for an animal, no one will fight for them.

What can everyone do about it? It is up to us to make the right choices and not contribute to the trade of sharks. We would never buy rhino horn or dolphin meat, and sharks are on that level of vulnerability. It is merely because we fear or hate them that these industries can get away with selling them and using them in our medicine and restaurants. It is up to consumers to question, taxpayers to voice their opinions and every individual to fight for an animal because all animals are important. Even if we fear sharks, we are a more dangerous species and what we hate and love determines what lives and what dies.

MADISON STEWART is an underwater filmmaker, PADI divemaster, TDI technical diver, ethical advisor, Sea Shepherd shark director, and delinquent.

After twenty years, I estimate
I've saved more than
twenty thousand paper towels.

Kristina Stockwood

What animal or environmental issue gets you out of bed, and why? I'm passionate about recycling, re-using, saving water and keeping my carbon footprint low. I've always linked environmentalism and animal rights together. As a student, I wrote stories for the university newspaper raising the ethics of testing products on animals – something there wasn't a lot of awareness about yet in the '80s. I made a pro-recycling film from the perspective of cats and dogs who were watching garbage pile up (with the alluring title *Erotic Dog Dreams*). My kids have been raised as vegetarians and when my daughter was four, we were talking about food and meat one day, after which she said, "Mommy, don't be silly. People don't EAT animals!" It was interesting to see how obvious it was to her that being a carnivore is not the default human condition.

What are you doing about it? Balancing. At work or going out, I balance my innate germophobia in public washrooms with my passionate environmentalism and carry my own hand towel with me everywhere. (I avoid using paper towels.) After twenty years, I estimate I've saved more than 20,000 paper towels, which is the equivalent of one or two trees. (Think of how many people live in North America – over half a billion – and start thinking about each one of them using up one or two trees worth of paper towels every twenty years.) I've also signed up for a local energy offset company; I pay a small fee on top of my energy bill each month to contribute natural source power to the grid. We don't usually use the car in the city and instead bike or walk most places.

What can everyone do about it? Carry your own reusable towel around, and bring your own containers for take-out food. Put recycling bins and compost bins all over your house. Stop using straws in your drinks. Kick the coffee pod habit and brew your own with a reusable filter. Turn off the lights when you leave the room. Don't flush the toilet every time you pee. Support alternative energy sources like solar or wind. Teach your kids to love the planet and all the animals on it – they rely on us humans not to screw it up for them.

KRISTINA STOCKWOOD is a human rights defender, women's rights activist, and environmentalist. She is the chair of the Advisory Board of the Gulf Center for Human Rights.

What animal or environmental issue gets you out of bed, and why? Honeybees. I love their birdlike faces, their furry coats, the way they care for each other in the hive. I love watching them delve into bright-colored blossoms and return home with their legs and bodies covered with pollen. I love honey. It embodies the flavor of the bees' unique landscapes. And honeybees are important. They pollinate approximately one-third of all the food we eat. But bees and many other pollinators are in decline as they face habitat reduction, ubiquitous pesticide use, and a host of other problems.

What are you doing about it? I ask farmers, beekeepers, scientists, ecologists, mead-makers, and artists – who are doing innovative work to help the bees – to tell me their stories and their strategies, which I then share with the world in my writing. I also spend time with students of all ages teaching them about our pollinators and our landscapes and about strategies to keep them healthy.

What can everyone do about it? You can help the bees by planting more flowers — especially flowers native to your region – and by not using pesticides or fungicides. Be sure to buy plants and seeds that are pesticide-free. Buy organic food as often as you can. Buy honey from your local beekeeper. Encourage your neighbors to stop using pesticides, too. Together we can make the world better for the pollinators and ourselves.

HEATHER SWAN has a PhD in English and an MFA in poetry from the University of Wisconsin–Madison where she currently teaches environmental literature and writing. A chapbook of her poems, The Edge of Damage, *was published by Parallel Press. Her nonfiction writing about bees has appeared in* Aeon *and* ISLE, *and is forthcoming in* Resilience. *Her new book* Healing Bees *will be out in Fall 2016. She is also a beekeeper.*

The success of this food justice movement relies on the energy, brilliance, and cutting-edge ideas of young people.

Bryant Terry

Bryant Terry

What animal or environmental issue gets you out of bed, and why? I'm concerned about the negative impact of our industrialized food system or communities of color and on the environment. We need to start a revolution. A handful of transnational corporations are effectively ruining the very foundations of our food system, negatively impacting our air, soil, and water. I have two daughters want to do all that I can to ensure that they have clean air to breathe, clean soil to grow healthy, sustainable food and clean water to drink. My daughters drive my passion to help people change their habits, attitudes, and politics around health food, and environmental issues.

What are you doing about it? Because many of us have been lulled to sleep by ou industrialized food system, I work at the grassroots level, collaborating with NGOs and community-based organizations. I talk about food insecurity, environmental racism and any number of issues that deal with health, food, and farming. I write cookbooks and lecture at universities and conferences. I feel strongly that the success of this food justice movement relies on the energy, brilliance, and cutting-edge ideas of young people. So I collaborate with schools and community organizations that work with young people and I use social media and pop culture as a way to inspire them to change their habits, attitudes, and politics.

What can everyone do about it? I advocate the 3 C's of change. As *consumers*, we must recognize that every purchase is a vote for the food system we want to see and the environment we want to live in; as *community* members, we must extend the conversation, engage and challenge our faith-based communities, long-standing community organizations, schools and work places to take part in improving our food system and the environment; and as *citizens*, we must step forward and take a stand in the development of our local, state, and national food policies.

BRYANT TERRY is a 2015 James Beard Leadership Award-winning chef and a national leader in the movement to promote healthy eating. He is the author of Afro-Vegan: Farm-Fresh African, Caribbean, and Southern Flavors Remixed; *the critically acclaimed V*egan Soul Kitchen; *and, along with co-author Anna Lappé,* Grub, *which the* New York Times *called "ingenious." Bryant's work has been featured in the* New York Times, Gourmet, Food & Wine, *and* O: The Oprah Magazine, *among others. He is currently the inaugural Chef-in-Residence a the Museum of the African Diaspora in San Francisco. He lives in Oakland, California.*

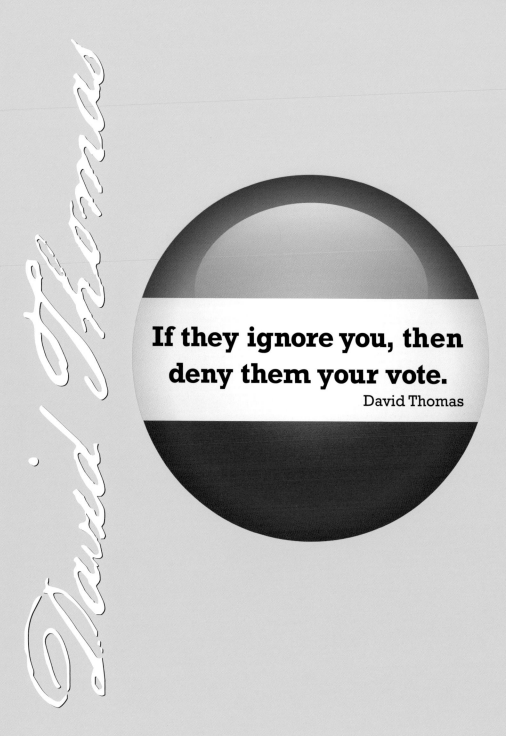

If they ignore you, then deny them your vote.

David Thomas

What animal or environmental issue gets you out of bed, and why? The forecast biodiversity losses not only get me out of bed, they give me nightmares. We're on the brink of a species apocalypse and our leaders don't seem to know or care. Some fifty terrestrial species and an undefined number of marine species have disappeared since Europeans came to Australia. Now over one hundred more are about to vanish. This "species Armageddon" is the result of cavalier development across our country. Some say the forecast losses are minor in biodiversity's grand scheme, but this is just a convenient evasion of responsibility for leaving a healthy natural heritage intact. It denies the potential for further medical remedies that may be derived from species research, especially marine research. It disallows the inner human health benefits that come from the wonder of a healthy ocean or species-filled bush. I'm a life-long bushwalker, boater, and recreational fisher. I revel in memories of the pleasure and spiritual renewal these pursuits have brought me. But with biodiversity loss, I fear my grandchildren will be denied the depth of experiences I've enjoyed. I'm not anti-development, but I am pro-science-based and exemplary planning that minimizes environmental harm and ensures that biodiversity remains intact.

What are you doing about it? With my wife, Barbara, I've created The Thomas Foundation. Its primary objective is to arrest the decline in Australia's biodiversity. Emphasis has been on terrestrial conservation, with the David Thomas Challenge delivering $28m to conservation organizations that have added 5.3m hectares to land under conservation management. Now we have shifted our focus to marine conservation, funding projects across Australian waters, especially on the Great Barrier Reef and Port Phillip Bay. Our goal is restoring the health of the bays and estuaries, including the restoration of natural oyster and mussel reefs. All these projects are working toward delivering biodiversity benefits.

What can everyone do about it? Badger your politicians at all levels of government. Tell them that all aspects of environmental protection are important and that ecological degradation is simply not acceptable to you. And if they ignore you, then deny them your vote. If enough of us do this, it will catch on.

*In 1998, **DAVID** and **BARBARA THOMAS** established The Thomas Foundation to pursue their long-held philanthropic interests. Their energies are focused on protecting Australia's biodiversity, marine conservation, marine parks, and Fight for the Reef campaign.*

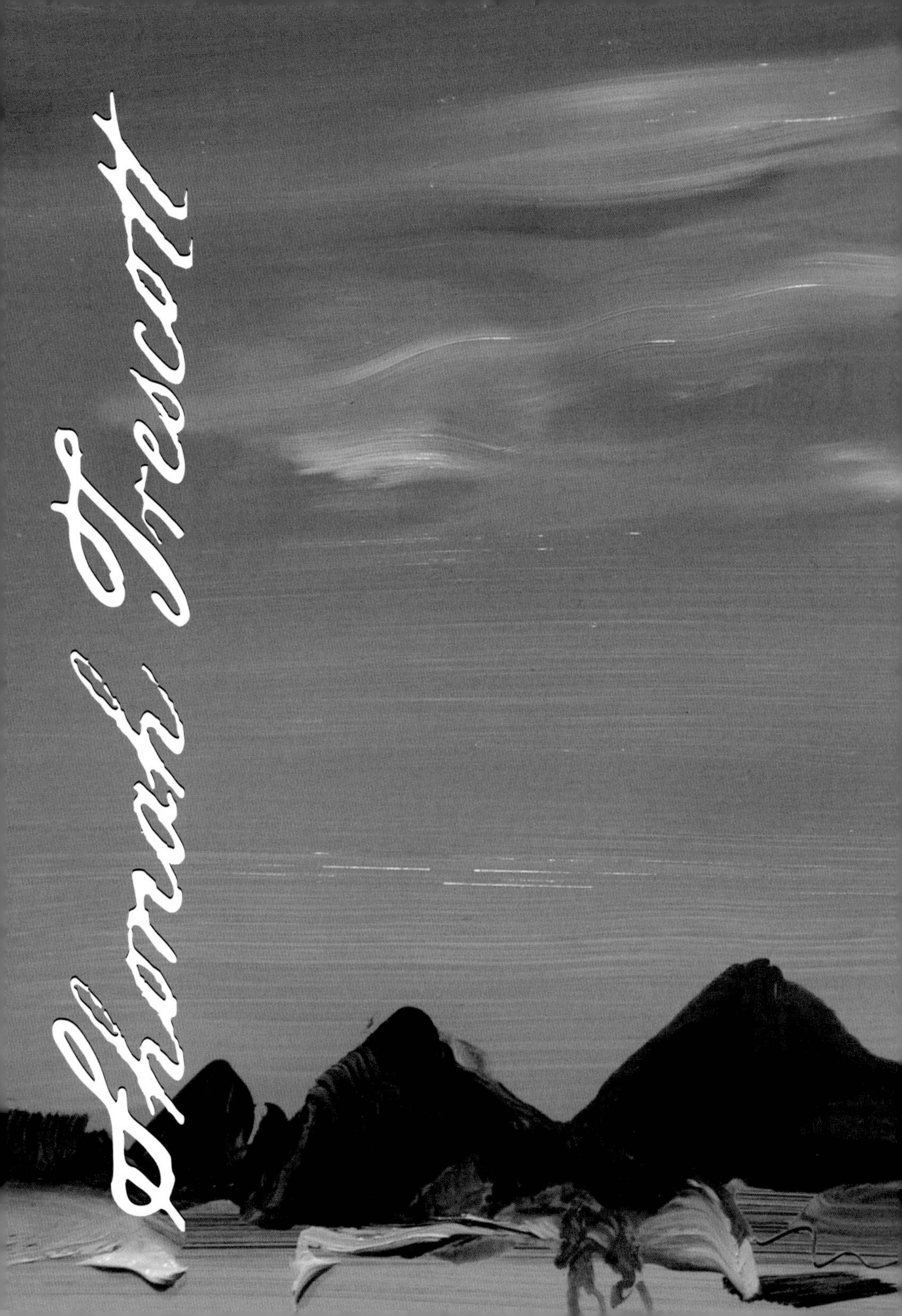
Shonah Prescott

What animal or environmental issue gets you out of bed, and why? The pressing issue of climate change and my desire to help preserve this beautiful world for all living things now and those to come gets me out of bed. I have always been involved and passionate about conservation of the natural world, but during the last four years, I have been working closely with climate change scientists in and out of the field. I have no doubt that the threat of climate change is real and urgent.

What are you doing about it? As an artist, my work is centered around the natural system we inhabit and how we relate to and use our environment and resources. My paintings invite people into a creative sphere – away from graphs, dry data and doom-and-gloom scenarios – where one can experience the visual politics of climate change in another way. I believe art can help to inspire audiences to approach environmental issues in positive ways. Aside from my artistic endeavors, I connect with individuals, groups, organizations, and institutions working to combat climate change. I have worked with the international scientific community in the Arctic and I often hold art workshops with local schools. I exhibit work in public places and create free public discussions on art, science, and climate change.

What can everyone do about it? Become an inspired shepherd of the planet. This is a decisive moment for humanity; our current course is not sustainable. Everyone can help by demanding better from our leaders and connecting ourselves to the issues. Become aware of and educate yourself about your immediate environment. Join communities who are working to implement change on both local and international levels. At home, plant a garden, recycle, re-use, pick up rubbish, buy local when possible, don't use plastic bags, support and become involved with environmental groups or create one in your community. Be positive in the call for action and inspired by the next generation who will inherit this planet we call home. We still have a small window of opportunity – it is now.

SHONAH TRESCOTT is an Australian artist specializing in environmental issues. She is presently based in Berlin, Germany. She exhibits internationally.

ALL LIVING CREATURES ARE OUR BROTHERS & SISTERS

Paul Rodney Turner

What animal or environmental issue gets you out of bed, and why? I have traveled the world, including visiting three war zones, and I've seen abuse of animals, humans, and the environment. It pains me that today the abuse continues to get worse. Minimizing this abuse inspires me to get out of bed every day especially because feel I have a viable solution.

What are you doing about it? I founded Food for Life Global to spearhead the expansion of Food for Life projects around the world. Our mission is to "create peace and prosperity in the world through the liberal distribution of pure plant-based meals prepared with loving intention." I have volunteered for this charity for the last 32 years and I intend to continue to drive that mission until I d   believe that as long as there is violence and spiritual inequality, there will never be peace in this world. If humans cannot value the spiritual essence of all beings then there is no hope of a united world.

What can everyone do about it? Take the time to contemplate the truth of spiritual equality and understand, as Saint Francis did, that all living creatures are our brothers and sisters. The key is to change the perception of our true nature from that of a mortal and fallible physical body to an infallible and dynamic spirit soul—the true seat of consciousness. I firmly believe this transformation of consciousness begins with mastering the tongue. You see, the tongue has two functions: tasting and vibrating. According to the ancient yoga tradition, by mastering the tongue we can master all the other senses, including the mind. It is also important to understand that food is the center of every culture (in fact, it defines the culture), and eating is something we do every day for health and social nourishment. Therefore, by eating only the purest plant-based foods that are free of violence, naturally harvested and prepared w   e and gratitude, and only speaking words that are truthful, encouraging and inspiring we can subsequently nourish our body, mind, and spirit and expand our awareness. I also feel strongly about the need for humans to reconnect with animals, for we have plenty to learn from them, and that is why my wife and I now run Juliana's Animal Sanctuary in Colombia. It is my personal mission to share this solution.

PAUL RODNEY TURNER, *the "food yogi," is currently the director of Food for Life Global, the world's largest vegan food-relief organization with projects in over sixty countries serving up to two million meals daily.*

Merlin Tuttle

What animal or environmental issue gets you out of bed, and why? Bats. Their ecological and economic contributions are essential to our well-being. From earliest childhood, I've been fascinated by nature. In high school, I discovered bats and learned from personal experience that the cave dwellers near my home were disappearing rapidly. Most people feared and hated bats as sources of rabies (despite the fact that almost no one ever contracted any disease from a bat). I discovered bats to be exceptionally gentle, intelligent, and beneficial, and couldn't resist telling others.

What are you doing about it? As a younger man, I limited my initial conservation efforts to the owners of bat caves where I conducted my graduate research. I was encouraged to see the landowners' perspectives shift from fearing and killing bats to liking and protecting them, but I remained far from optimistic about helping bats in general. I never even imagined that I, personally, could make a difference, nonetheless, in 1982, with both encouragement and resistance, I founded Bat Conservation International. Against all odds, BCI grew rapidly. By the time I retired from leadership 30 years later, BCI had educated millions of people worldwide, people who now appreciate and protect bats. We sponsored research and conservation projects, and were instrumental in gaining long-term protection for thousands of key habitats, including a national park in American Samoa and the most important remaining bat caves of North America. It's progress that will stand the test of time.

What can everyone do about it? Be passionate. There is no greater old-age reward than knowing your life has been well lived and that you're still able to change the world for the better, especially on behalf of a cause you love. If you wish to take pride in extraordinary achievement, focus on important causes that don't already appeal to the masses – they provide wonderful opportunities. You don't have to be a leader to take pride in making a big difference. Every leader needs help, and even small contributions of time or resources can add up to be crucial, especially for causes that are not yet popular. Finally, be responsible by ensuring that your contributions are used wisely; don't just give to broad, emotional appeals without checking on results.

MERLIN TUTTLE is an ecologist, wildlife photographer, and conservationist who studies bats and champions their preservation. He founded Bat Conservation International (BCI), an organization devoted to research, education and conservation of bats in 1982. He also founded Merlin Tuttle's Bat Conservation in support of his continuing efforts.

What animal or environmental issue gets you out of bed, and why? We are currently living through the sixth mass extinction event on this planet. All around us, species that evolved over millions of years are quietly disappearing, often without us even noticing. While past mass extinctions have been caused by events such as asteroid strikes, today's is caused by the combined and varied impacts of human life – it is almost entirely an anthropogenic extinction event, with some human communities having a more significant impact than others.

What are you doing about it? I am a philosopher and anthropologist. I explore how extinction matters differently to different communities, and how we might better respond to this pressing challenge. At the moment, I'm researching a range of critically endangered species, including the beautiful Hawaiian Crow (or 'alalā), which now lives only in captivity. I write books and articles and I teach university students about these issues. I also try to help people directly involved in conservation programs think about how they might work in other, hopefully better, ways. Writing and teaching are vital components of the deeper cultural change required to make a long-lasting difference. They're also creative practices that I greatly enjoy.

What can everyone do about it? One of the particular challenges – and opportunities – of the present moment is that the diverse environmental and animal issues that concern us are so tightly entangled with one another and with our daily lives: the food we eat, the clothes we wear, how we get to work. Each of us has a broad range of attachment sites we can use either to enable the continuation of destructive practices or to challenge them. I encourage people to find ways of getting involved (directly or indirectly, however big or small) that fascinate and inspire them. It is important that the change we bring about in the world is grounded in passionate and creative practices that don't just address one issue in isolation, but that enact the broader relationships, practices and ultimately the world we want for the future.

THOM VAN DOOREN is a senior lecturer in environmental humanities at the University of New South Wales in Sydney, Australia and the co-editor of the international, open-access journal Environmental Humanities. *He is currently a Humboldt Research Fellow at the Rachel Carson Center for Environment and Society in Munich. His research and writing focuses on some of the many philosophical, ethical, cultural, and political issues that arise in the context of species extinctions.*

Paul Watson

What animal or environmental issue gets you out of bed, and why? If the ocean dies, we all die. We cannot survive on a planet with dead oceans. I defend biodiversity in the ocean by enforcing international conservation law and advocating anti-poaching. I will do all I can to protect ecological integrity on the planet we call Earth. (Although, more correctly, our planet should be called Ocean).

What are you doing about it? In 1972, I co-founded the Greenpeace Foundation then went on to found the Sea Shepherd Conservation Society. Today Sea Shepherd is a global movement. We intercept and shut down illegal whalers, fishing operations and marine wildlife exploiters. We practice aggressive non-violence and regard the camera as our most powerful weapon. We use the media to get our message across and created the popular Animal Planet television show *Whale Wars*. We initiated Operation Vortex, a campaign to remove plastic from the sea. We recruit volunteers from around the world to directly participate in our activities, thus providing a conduit for people to put their passion, courage, and imagination into action.

What can everyone do about it? We need to stop eating the ocean. There are too many people and not enough fish. A great percentage of the fish caught is converted to animal feed – fishmeal to provide feed for pigs, chickens, domestic cats, etc. Adopt a vegan diet – no meat, no fish, no eggs, no dairy products. Stop using plastic. Carry your own shopping bags and try to buy products not contained or wrapped in plastic. Choose to live a plastic-free, low energy, organic vegan lifestyle. It may be more expensive but it beats the alternative – the death of our ocean. People can also support Sea Shepherd with contributions not just of funds but also with their own involvement as volunteer crew.

*An author and activist, **CAPTAIN PAUL WATSON** helms the Sea Shepherd Conservation Society, the world's most active marine protection nonprofit organization. He has participated in campaigns to protect the oceans and marine biodiversity – from plankton to the great whales. He is dedicated to the research, investigation, and enforcement of laws, treaties, resolutions, and regulations established to protect marine wildlife and their habitats worldwide. In between campaigns, Watson writes and lectures extensively at universities and events around the world. He has published six books and was noted by* Time *magazine as one of the environmental heroes of the 20th Century in the year 2000.*

Kimberley Wells

What animal or environmental issue gets you out of bed, and why? The welfare status of working horses, donkeys, and mules is my alarm clock. It's unavoidable that equines have to work, but their welfare is vital. No animal should suffer, nor fail to be recognized and valued for their contribution to a community or society. In the developing world, some people depend on these animals to survive and improve their lives. Equine owners may lack the knowledge, skills, motivation, and/or supporting systems to care for and meet their animals' needs. I'm motivated to address these problems. Positive changes for animals are possible, and that's where I come in.

What are you doing about it? As the senior welfare advisor for the Brooke Hospital for Animals, my role is to make learning about animal welfare easier, as this is often a new concept to some people in countries where we work. We are empowering local people to better the lives of these hard working animals in Asia, Africa, Latin America, and the Middle East. From providing alternatives to harmful traditional handling and treatments to showing owners how to understand and communicate with their animals, our teams and local health providers are improving how equines are cared for, managed, and used now and for the future.

What can everyone do about it? People are often unaware that their daily decisions can affect animal's lives. You do not need to be an expert in animal science to be an animal advocate and driver for change. In fact, equipped with the right information and empathy, public demand can be a key driver for animal welfare improvements. With 112 million working equine animals in the developing world, it's likely that you will come into contact with one used for tourism. For example, a horse pulling a carriage, mules carrying your luggage, and donkeys carrying you. Take a closer look and before you use the animal consider if the animal is fit and healthy, ask how their basic needs are met and report any concerns.

KIMBERLY'S background and formal qualifications have been in animal bioscience, applied animal behavior and welfare science, veterinary nursing, and adult education. She began her practical work at her local animal shelter, and continued to gain practical experience through varied animal establishments. Her experience, education and eagerness to improve animal welfare internationally led her leave her American roots in order to fulfill her ambition of working in the UK for the Brooke. She aspires to write a children's book series to engage future generations in compassionate care for animals.

Elizabeth Mere

What animal or environmental issue gets you out of bed, and why? Increasing access to drinking water. It is easy to take for granted the daily pleasures of having water at one's convenience. Worldwide, it is estimated that 980 million people do not have access to safe water. Among the statistics are real people and communities I work with. Every day, they spend up to three hours in search of water, often returning with murky water infested with disease. The poor, especially in urban areas, pay up to ten times more per unit of water compared with people with house connections. In several cases, there have also been reported incidences of girls dropping out of school and others being sexually harassed due to lack of water and improved sanitation facilities. There are people in every community who do not have access to safe water. In Los Angeles and Sydney, there are homeless people who need access to a shower. Among the First Nations in Canada, native tribes in the U.S., and aboriginals' reserves, lack of water challenges community health. Access to reliable and safe water reduces exposure to contamination and disease thereby improving health and well-being.

What are you doing about it? I work with local microfinance institutions and non-governmental organizations (NGOs) to develop water loan products for households earning above $1.25 a day. This enables households currently without water to acquire a water asset of their own. I have been successful in providing technical expertise and mentorship to local partners, fostering continued quality improvement, and delivering high-quality products to clients and communities. I see firsthand how lives in communities are transformed because of improved access to safe water.

What can everyone do about it? Learn about water scarcity in your region and also around the world. Start campaigns and petitions to urge governments to take more responsibility for providing efficient services and providing an enabling environment to increase access to water for all. Development agencies should focus on providing sustainable solutions. Individual could consider contributing technical expertise in improving efficiency and effectiveness of development projects. Practice water saving tips in your house.

LIZ WERE is an accomplished program manager and certified process specialist working with MFIs and NGOs in Africa to improve water and sanitation coverage. When she is not working, she explores, enjoys hiking though mountains and diving around the world.

IT'S A CASE OF GOING FORWARD AND NOT GOING BACKWARD.

Dr. Mary White

Dr. Mary White

What animal or environmental issue gets you out of bed, and why? Worrying about the future of the human race and hoping that my grandchildren and great grandchildren have some sort of a future. And also feeling that if more people – if everybody – became interested in doing what is necessary to stop things like climate change. If we have everybody working on it, we can make a difference. And even if we've only got hundreds of thousands of people thinking the right sort of thought, we can virtually change atmospheres and we can achieve things that we've never dreamed of. That is very important to me.

What are you doing about it? I use my writing to bring messages of hope. Everything that I write carries a message of hope and action. If people are thoroughly depressed about what they hear, they tend to shut their ears to everything. If we can't do anything to make it better, then we can just eat, drink, and be merry for tomorrow we die. I don't feel like that. I feel we have a huge responsibility and I've always tried to take my share of that. I still have people who write to me and say, "You were the one who my son spoke too when he was ten and he suddenly became interested in all these things to do with geology, and earth history, and evolution, and all these sort of things."

What can everyone do about it? Spread the message. Every single one of us has the ability to do things that are going to be useful. And what's more, it isn't necessarily expensive. We mustn't think about it as a financial thing, but I think every individual in a world has an absolute duty to do something about it. We should counteract the tremendous waste. We need to have a very different attitude about everything. Reuse. Recycle. Share. Help. It's a case of going forward and not going backward.

A conservationist, paleobotanist, and environmental educator, **DR. WHITE** *is also the author of many books including* The Greening of Gondwana *and* Earth Alive. *Her lifetime ambition has been to protect biodiversity and promote a love and interest in our natural world. When she was seventy-seven years old, Dr. White purchased and established the eighty-three-hectare Falls Forest Retreat as a permanently protected biodiversity sanctuary. At eighty-nine years old, Dr. White is currently working on her autobiography.*

What animal or environmental issue gets you out of bed, and why? Every day, I draw inspiration from my ranger colleagues, their families, and communities. Against huge odds and grave danger, they get themselves up daily to protect and give their all for something much bigger than themselves – Nature. Who among us can really say we would give our life for that of a mountain gorilla, a tiger, an elephant, or a forest? The word "hero" is used a lot but I think history will show that these protectors of nature, our rangers, are the real heroes of the planet, in the truest sense of the word.

What are you doing about it? I fit my piece of the puzzle into a growing band of supporters. It's easy to be overwhelmed by all that's happening, but my focus is on respecting the rangers we place on the frontline of conservation by raising awareness of their critical work. With that, we raise support for ranger training, equipping, and their basic human rights. We've helped train hundreds of rangers and equipped many more. We've supported over 150 widows of rangers killed, but there are 900 more waiting for support. With on average 100 more rangers killed every year, there's much more to do. I'm seeing a growing voice and support for our rangers, so I remain hopeful, focused, and determined.

What can everyone do about it? Find your piece of the puzzle, connect it to other pieces, or help others realize a piece they are putting into place. If you are passionate about something, you're more likely to push through the hardships to make a difference. Find that thing (or things) that you're passionate about, join others with that same passion, marry it with some smarts, and other people of integrity, and go for it – you can and will make a difference, and if not, well you can look yourself in the mirror and the next generation in the eye and say I tried.

SEAN WILLMORE is a former Australian park ranger. He is the founder and managing director of the Thin Green Line Foundation and the president of the International Rangers Federation (a nonprofit organization made up of 70+ ranger associations in 50 countries), both established to raise awareness of and support the critical work that the world's park rangers do in conserving our natural and cultural heritage. Sean carries his message to business and government leaders, schools, and community groups and continues to create awareness and delivery of critical support for the park rangers on the front-line of conservation.

Acknowledgements

First and foremost we'd like to thank our incredible contributors, thank you so much for your insights, inspiration, and dedication to making the planet a better place. And to Rosalie Kunoth-Monks, our sincerest gratitude for gracing us with the foreword for the book, we are honored.

Thanks to our great team: Luke Jarman for his brilliant design and complete faith in this project, Karen Stevenson for her tireless efforts in editing the book, Vivien Valk for her design and production expertise, Jane Price for her editorial input, Barbara Greenberg for her great copy editing. Thanks as well to all our photographers and illustrators for your beautiful work. Also to Carrick Wilke, Jean Schroeder and Mary Heim our Australian and US printers, Diana Horner for doing the eBook, Alex Kislaitis for jumping on the website at short notice, and Clarissa Soriano for always providing great transcriptions. Thanks too to all the people behind the scenes working with our contributors, you all know who you are-you who put up with the tireless emails, constant requests, helped us out enormously.

A huge thank you to our Planet donors; Michele, Mark and Honi Kellner, Natasha and Ted Lilly Family, Deborah Ann Zorn, Mark and Mary Bookman, and Jeanie Pollack, Joe and Melissa Cox – we could not have done this without you.

Thanks to Gloria Jarman, Issy, Johnno, Kirstie, Steve Bennett, Sue Cato, Jane Tewson, Craig McIntosh, Rebecca Newman, Mark Rudder, Virginia del Giudice, Liz Tormes, Barbara Fougere, Elizabeth D'Avingdor, Sandy Peacock. And Matthew, Sean and Sophie Gies for their calm support and unwavering belief in the power of the planet to guide us all on the right path. The staff, clients and patients at the Royal Treatment for their everyday heroism in dealing with matters of health and heart. All our families and friends - human and furry, and especially our beautiful planet – there are no words to express our sincerest gratitude for everything you provide us with, every single day.

Proceeds from this book support charities directly represented by contributors and fund a multi-media awareness campaign about other planet heroes in the world.

Reference

Ababu, Shikerke
botanicaethiopia.com/tag/
etse-fewus-association

Ahern, Pam
edgarsmission.org.au

Balcombe, Jonathan
jonathanbalcombe.com
humanesociety.org

Beatley, Tim
biophiliccities.org

Beattie, Sport
gamerangersinternational.org

Becker, Karen
drkarenbecker.com

Bekoff, Marc
marcbekoff.com
ethologicalethics.org

Biggi, Emanuele
anura.it

Bodkin, Frances
dharawalstories.com

Branson, Richard
virgin.com
globalgoals.org

Brinkman, Baba
bababrinkman.com

Budet, Osvaldo
osvaldobudet.com

Burrows, Victoria
starpawsrescue.org

Burton, Natasha
balistreetdogs.org.au

Cameron, Jonah
Facebook: Jonah's Forest
Friends
orangutan.or.id

Campagna, Claudio
wcs.org

Casteel, Seth
littlefriendsphoto.com
onepicturesaves.com

Chhabra, Rohan
rohan-chhabra.com
re-culture.com

Collet, Carole
designandlivingsystems.com

Cowlishaw, Teagan
aarlifashion.com

Dankovich, Theresa
drinkablebook.tilt.com

Day, Ashley
vtrsolutions.com
futurefighters.org

Day, Charles
thelookinglass.com

de Groot, Laurens
shadowview.org

Dorji, Dechen
wwfbhutan.org.bt

Douglas, Ian
vetsbeyondborders.org

Doust, Kelly
thecraftyminx.com.au

Durie, Jamie
jamiedurie.com

Earle, Sylvia
mission-blue.org

Elliot, Rosemary
sentientorg.wix.com

Fasseas, Alexis
pawschicago.org

Galiana, Pauline
paulinegaliana.com

Gilmore, Peter
quay.com.au

Goodall, Jane
janegoodall.org

Gouby, Mélanie
melanie-gouby.com

Grandin, Temple
templegrandin.com

Habib, Rodney
rodneyhabib.com

Hansen, Erik
GoGreenOhio.org

Hawken, Paul
paulhawken.com
drawdown.org

Hewson, John
aodproject.net

Hill, Graham
lifeedited.com

Holland, Jennifer
cuttlefishprose.com

Houghton, Natalie
brightfutureenterprises.com.au

Hunter, Melita
songsaa.com
songsaafoundation.org

Hutagalung, Nadya
letelephantsbeelephants.org
un-grasp.org

Jordan, Chris
chrisjordan.com

Knell, Gary E.
nationalgeographic.com

Kortenhorst, Jules
rmi.org
carbonwarroom.com

Lameman, Ron
raventrust.com

Locke, Harvey
y2y.net
natureneedshalf.org

Longstaff, Simon
ethics.org.au

Louv, Richard
childrenandnature.org
richardlouv.com

Manson, Shirley
garbage.com

Martin, Mandy
mandy-martin.com
arnhembrand.com

Martinez, Juan
childrenandnature.org

McArthur, Jo-Anne
weanimals.org

McIntosh, Derek
nationalregisterofbigtrees.com.au
bushcare.org.au
treeproject.org.au

McIntyre, Jo
jomcintyre.com

Münter, Leilani
leilani.green

Murrell, Frances
madge.org.au

Natterson-Horowitz Dr. B.
zoobiquity.com

O'Brien, Robyn
robynobrien.com

Oelwang, Jean
virgin.com/unite

Palmquist, Rick
ahvmf.org

Peterman, Audrey
legacyontheland.com

Philip, Radika
lt.lk

Platner, Jill
jillplatner.com

Polsinelli, Jasmine
jasminepolsinelli.blogspot.ca

Pouliot, Alison
alisonpouliot.com

Pratzky, Dayne
frackmanthemovie.com

Psihoyos, Louie
opsociety.org

Rands, Malcolm
ecoman.co.nz

Reid, Craig
african-parks.org

Ridgeway, Rick
patagonia.com

Rosenthal, Nancy
nywildfilmfestival.com

Ruxton, Jo
plasticoceans.net

Sahtouris, Elisabet
sahtouris.com

Schepers, Frans
rewildingeurope.com

Sengupta, Alokparna
hsi.org
leapingbunny.org

Sheldrick, Angela
sheldrickwildlifetrust.org

Shepard, Peggy
weact.org

Sherman, Brian
voiceless.org.au

Skiff, Jennifer
jenniferskiff.com

Sommerville-Knott, Holly
holleysomerville.com

Stewart, Madison
madisonstewart.com.au

Terry, Bryant
bryant-terry.com

Thomas, David
thomasfoundation.org.au

Trescott, Shonah
shonahtrescott.com

Turner, Paul Rodney
ffl.org
julianasfarm.org/en

Tuttle, Merlin
merlintuttle.org

van Dooren, Thom
thomvandooren.org
environmentalhumanities.org

Watson, Paul
seashepherd.org

Wells, Kimberly
thebrooke.org

Were, Liz
water.org

Willmore, Sean
thingreenline.org.au

Photos and Art

127 Hugo Sharp **129**Juan Martinez **130**Jo-Anne McArthur / We Animals/ **131**Kyle Behrend/Edgar's Mission **132**Natasha Milne **134**illustration/ McIntyre... Countdown...collage 2008 Life on our planet hangs by a thread **138**Natasha Milne**140**bigstock-Blace-faced-monkey-grey-langu-46239736 **141**Joanna Brooks **143**Darcy Sherman/Sassafras Photography **144**corbis 42-26234354 **145**Chris Willan **147**Judy Francesconi Photography **148**iStock_000017028675 **149**The Heinz Awards **150**Darshana Abraham **151**Radhika Philip **152/153**Ryan Slack **156**Alison Pouliot **157**Valerie Chetelat **158**Max Phillips **160/161**Oceanic Preservation Society **162**Natasha Milne **164**Jcd Bird **166**ThinkstockPhotos-127016876 **168**Donnie Heddon/Patagonia **172**David Jones **173**Jess Hickie **175**Philip La Vere **176**Staffan Widstrand/Rewilding Europe **178**Maria Robledo **180**illustration/ Angela Sheldrick **181**Robert Carr-Hartley **182**bigstock-Manhattan-Roof-Gardens-Editor-94509647 **183**Jim Harrison **184**'Chook Heaven' oil on canvas board 2006 by Jo McIntyre **189**Lady Juliette photography **190/191**Ernst Stewart**194**iStock_000067049517 **197**Reprinted with permission from Afro-Vegan by Bryant Terry, copyright (c) 2014. Published by Ten Speed Press, a division of Penguin Random House, Inc. Photography (c) 2014 by Paige Green **200**painting by Shonah Trescott **204**Merlin Tuttle **206**'Sanguine moon' woodblock print by Margaret Barnaby **208**canstockphoto1375334 **209**Sea Shepherd **210**Natasha Milne **212**iStock_000049215134 **216**Sean Wilmore **224**Milne/Mel Koutchavlis, Royal/Kerry Bolger **Bkgnd image** bigstock-Great-for-textures-and-backgro-14120999 **BK COVER**iStock_000028827608

About the editors

NATASHA MILNE In addition to her professional work, Natasha is a volunteer at her local wildlife rescue organization. She has just begun a pilot program with local schools aimed at reconnecting children with nature through the creative use of technology. A photographer and fine artist for over twenty years both in New York and abroad, Natasha's clients include the UN Development Project in Mali, West Africa, Canon, Condé Nast, and MSL. Her work has been sold, exhibited and auctioned internationally. Natasha is on a mission to dedicate the remainder of her life to the welfare and care of our beautiful planet, and all her creatures. She lives in Sydney, Australia with her husband Luke, step-daughters, Amy and Bella, and two girl dogs called Fred and Charlie.

DR. BARBARA ROYAL Internationally renowned integrative veterinarian, lecturer and author, Dr. Royal is the founder of The Royal Treatment Veterinary Center in Chicago. A passionate advocate of common sense and cutting-edge approaches to animal health, Barbara provides a bridge between Western and Eastern medicine. She is the current president of the American Holistic Veterinary Medical Foundation (AHVMF) and past president of the American Holistic Veterinary Medical Association (AHVMA), and is on the Board of Directors for PAWSChicago, one of the largest no-kill shelters in the country. Information and stories from her recent book, *The Royal Treatment: A Natural Approach to Wildly Healthy Pets,* have been featured on radio, TV, and online globally. Her countless devoted patients and clients include Oprah Winfrey and Billy Corgan. She lives in Chicago with her husband Matthew, children, Sean and Sophie, and an assortment of wildly healthy pets.